JAZZ PIANO
CONCEPTS & TECHNIQUES

by JOHN VALERIO

ISBN 978-0-7935-7175-8

HAL•LEONARD® CORPORATION

7777 W. BLUEMOUND RD. P.O. BOX 13819 MILWAUKEE, WI 53213

Visit Hal Leonard Online at
www.halleonard.com

C O N T E N T S

PREFACE

This book offers a straightforward step-by-step approach to learning how to play basic piano realizations of jazz and pop tunes from lead sheets. The focus is on chords, chord voicings, harmony, melody and accompaniment, and styles. One with no knowledge of jazz piano playing can learn from this book since the most elementary chord voicings and procedures are presented first. The more advanced player can use the book to review and catalogue voicing systems as well as learn new ones.

The book offers several systems for voicing chords and methodical ways of practicing each system. As the book progresses, systems are combined and more elaborate systems are introduced. The concluding lessons demonstrate professional approaches to keyboard realizations of standard types of tunes.

This is not a jazz theory book, but basic jazz theory can be learned here. Chord substitutions, embellishments of chord progressions, melodic improvisation, etc. are not covered in this book. The basic foundation in jazz keyboard playing presented here offers workable solutions to the problems inherent in spontaneously playing stylistically viable piano arrangements from a lead sheet. Other aspects of jazz theory can easily be applied once the material in this book is learned.

The lessons proceed from the simple to the complex and the material should be learned in the order presented. The more advanced student may skip to the later chapters, but it is suggested that he or she quickly review the early lessons first in order to learn the basic methodology of the book.

The book proceeds by presenting certain chord voicings and voicing formulas first. These are then applied to tunes. The voicing formulas are simple voice leading procedures that work well within common chord progresssions. Various ways of practicing each voicing and formula are demonstrated. Once a voicing and a voicing formula are used within the context of a tune, new voicings and formulas are introduced and then combined with older ones. One who has learned all of the voicings and formulas in the book will have a varied and flexible repertoire of arranging methods at his or her command.

It is assumed that the reader knows the most basic music theory. Major and minor scales should be known in all keys. A knowledge of the other modes is also helpful. Triads, seventh, and sixth chords should be known and understood. A knowledge of extended and altered chords is also helpful. The introduction will cover the basic theory necessary in order to proceed with the following lessons.

INTRODUCTION

Traditional music theory treats the triad (a three note chord) as the basic harmonic unit. The four basic triad types are shown below.

Fig. I-1

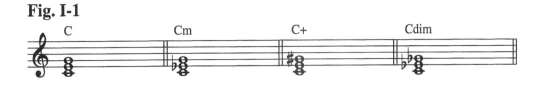

In traditional music theory a fourth note added to a triad is considered as an addition to the triad and is treated as such in various ways. Jazz theory treats four note chords as fundamental units of harmony. Thus, seventh and sixth chords are the norm. All further extensions of the seventh chord (ninths, elevenths, and thirteenths) are considered as additions.

The first part of this book will concentrate on seventh and sixth chords before dealing with these extensions. Fig. I-2 lists all of the basic four note chords required for the beginning chapters. These should be known by the student before undertaking the succeeding exercises. There are ten different chord types or qualities. The example below lists each chord type for the root C. All of the examples and exercises in the book will be based on these chord qualities. Extensions and alterations to them should be understood as additions to the basic seventh or sixth chord.

Fig. I-2

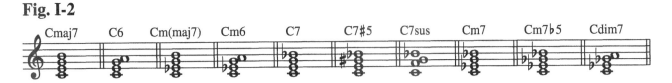

Seventh chords can be inverted to other positions. Below is an example for a C7 chord. All inversions should be known. The book deals primarily with root position and second inversion seventh chords.

Fig. I-2A

The tonal language used in most jazz and popular music is based on diatonic scales. Major and minor scales are most often used. These are seven note scales that alternate whole and half steps in different orders. There is one major scale that can start on each different note, thus there are twelve major scales for twelve major keys. There are three different minor scales, however, that can start on each different note, thus it derives thirty-six different scales for twelve minor keys. The three forms of the minor scale are the natural minor, the harmonic minor, and the melodic minor. The Appendix (page 135) lists all of the major and minor scales.

The notes of any particular scale generate chords that function as harmonic units within the framework of a key. These chords are produced by adding thirds (derived from the scale itself) above the scale tones which serve as roots of the chords. Traditional tonal music considers two added notes (a total of three notes) as a fundamental harmonic unit. These three note chords are referred to as triads. The chords generated by a scale relate to each other in consistent and predictable ways. Whereas the scale degrees of a scale are referred to by numbers - 1,2,3 etc., the chords generated from the scale degrees are referred to by Roman numerals - I, II, III, etc. Below are the basic triads in the key of C major.

Fig. I-3

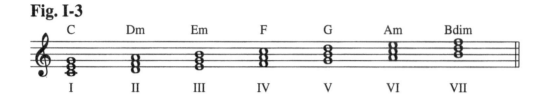

Different chord qualities are generated from different scale degrees. The I, IV and V chords are major triads, the II, III, and VI chords are minor triads, and the VII chord is a diminished triad.

More thirds can be added above the triadic structures. The addition of one more third will produce a seventh chord with four notes. Jazz theory uses the seventh chord as a point of departure. Below are the seventh chords generated from the C major and F major scales. Seventh chords generated from a major scale are referred to as Diatonic Seventh Chords. See the Appendix (page 144) for all of the Diatonic Seventh Chords in major.

Fig. I-4

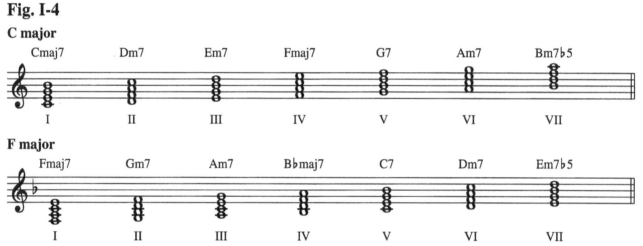

Different seventh chord qualities result from the diatonic seventh chord process. The I and IV chords are major seventh chords, the II, III, and VI chords are minor seventh chords, the V chord is a dominant seventh chord, and the VII chord is a minor seventh flat five chord (the same as a half-diminished seventh chord). The qualities are the same for identical scale degrees in all major keys. A I chord is always a major seventh chord, a II chord is always a minor seventh chord, a V chord is always a dominant seventh chord, etc. Chords function and relate to each other within the context of a key. Fmaj7 functions as the I chord in the key of F major, but as a IV chord in the key of C major. Dmin7 is the II chord in C major and the VI chord in F major. Within any given tune, keys can change often regardless of the key signature, and an awareness of chord functions and patterns can indicate when there is a key change.

In most situations, major and minor sixth chords can substitute for major seventh chords and minor-major seventh chords. A C6 is often used instead of, or immediately after, a Cmaj7 chord: Cmaj7 - C6. A minor sixth chord is often used instead of, or immediately after, a Cm(maj7) chord: Cm(maj7) - Cm6. Many of the examples in this book will employ two versions of I chords, i.e. Cmaj7 - C6.

A knowledge of Diatonic Seventh Chords in all major and minor keys is essential to understanding the relationship among chords. Understanding the relationships among chords is fundamental to playing jazz piano. This book presents a *form follows function* approach. Chords are voiced according to how they function and the performer, through practice, should naturally perceive the relationships within a chord progression and voice the chords accordingly without much thought. Different voicings and voicing formulas are isolated to concentrate on one procedure at a time in order to create "voicing habits." Once these habits are learned the player can use any one particular system at will and eventually create new ones.

Each chord quality can only function in a few different ways. The placement of a specific chord within a chord progression can usually signal what that function is, and thus the key at any particular moment can usually be inferred by the context of a grouping of chords. By limiting ourselves to the diatonic seventh chords shown in Fig. I-4 we can limit the possible functions of each chord quality. For instance, a major seventh chord can only be a I chord or a IV chord, a minor seventh chord can only be a II, III, or a VI chord, a dominant seventh chord can only be a V chord, and a minor seventh ♭5 can only be a VII chord or a II chord in minor. Although major and minor 6th chords are not strictly part of the diatonic 7th chord system, they can freely substitute for major and minor-major 7th chords. Usually the context of any particular chord type will "give away" its function and thus its key. There are exceptions, but the player will recognize these through experience.

The following example presents a simple chord progression. Each chord functions in the key of C major. There are no modulations to other keys and the progression can be analyzed in the key of C major as follows: I-VI-II-V-III-VI-II-V.

Fig. I-5

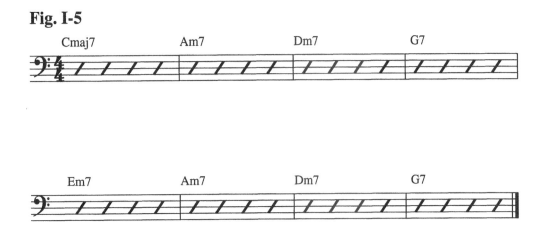

The next example presents a common chord progression that actually goes through several keys.

Fig. I-6

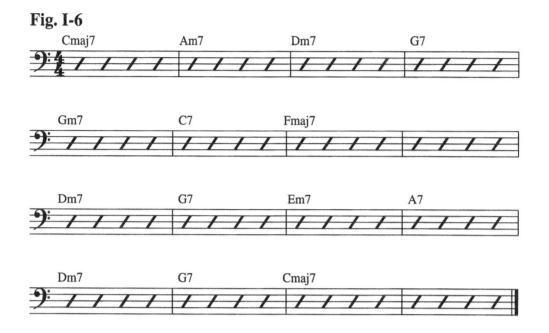

The context of each chord within the chord progression should be apparent. The first four measures function as I-VI-II-V in the key of C major. The Dm7 is clearly a II chord since it precedes its obvious V chord in C major. II and V chords are most often coupled in this way. The Am7 functions as a VI chord in this context since it is preceded by a I chord and followed by a II chord. This is a common progression and the key and chord function should be clear. The Am7, for example, does not in any way relate as a II chord in the key of G major or as a III chord in F major in this setting.

Measures 5 through 8 present a progression that does not relate to the key of C major and indicates a key change has been made to F major. Gm7 - C7 - Fmaj7 fucntion as II-V-I in F major. The next four measures present some ambiguity that leads to alternative interpretations of chord function. This kind of ambiguity gives tonal music its special quality. The Dm7 of measure 9 is coupled with "its" V chord, G7, and this would indicate a modulation back to C major for these two measures. Dm7, however, can also be thought of as a VI chord in F major when it is first heard after the Fmaj7 chord. The improviser can interpret the Dm7 either way or can purposely leave the situation ambiguous by avoiding notes that define one key over the other. A chord in this situation is known as a pivot chord since it can function in two different keys simultaneously. The G7 chord erases the ambiguity of the Dm7 since it clearly functions as V in the key of C major.

Measures 11 and 12 raise a similar problem with the Em7 being a III chord in C major and a II chord coupled with its V chord of D major. The A7 chord may also be considered a V chord in the key of Dminor. The last four measures bring us back again to C major. The procedures applied in the book will make one well aware of harmonic functions.

Minor keys present some special problems due to adjustments usually made to a minor scale. A clear-cut system of diatonic chords in minor is not really possible. Below are the diatonic seventh chords most often used in minor for the key of C minor.

Fig. I-7

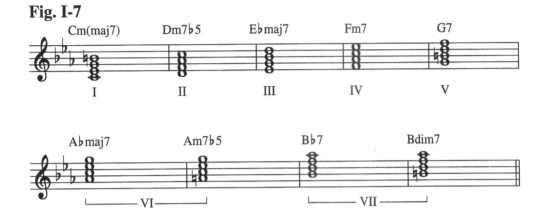

Note that there are two kinds of VI and VII chords. It is important to know that a I chord in minor should usually be a minor (major7) or a minor 6 chord, a II chord is usually a min7♭5 chord and a V chord is usually a dominant 7th chord. The Appendix (page 142) lists Diatonic Seventh Chords for all minor keys.

All basic aspects of jazz theory are presented in this book and the novice can acquire a solid theoretical foundation through the practical application of theoretical concepts to jazz keyboard performance.

The formulaic approach used for this book is one that fosters automatic responses to typical harmonic situations. The tunes written for the book are meant to sound like other tunes and contain typical chord progressions used in many jazz and pop standards. The lessons proceed by isolating one voicing system and voicing formula at a time. Each is applied to tunes before a new system and formula are introduced. Systems are combined along the way.

It is important to practice the exercises in the order given. Chords in the right hand and roots in the left hand are often practiced before melodies are included in order to establish the harmonic progression and root movement in the player's ear and fingers. Practicing in the given order is the easiest and most efficient way to learning the material. Most of the lessons presented in the book are derived from previous ones and one can quickly proceed from one to the other without much difficulty. The reader should apply all of the techniques and principles in the book to his or her favorite tunes. Lead sheets for all of the tunes referred to are in the Appendix.

SECTION 1
LESSON 1
DIATONIC SEVENTH CHORDS

The following exercises illustrate four ways of practicing diatonic seventh chords in close position. A close-position chord is a chord voicing that uses all adjacent chord tones without any skips between tones. The exercises should be practiced in all **twelve major keys.** Each exercise is written in the keys of C and G major. The student should continue for the remaining major keys. While any order of keys will suffice for these exercises, it is suggested that the student use the following order of major keys based on increasing sharps and flats: C, G, F, D, B♭, A, E♭, E, A♭, B, D♭, G♭.

The student should practice the exercises in the order given for each key before proceeding to the next key. The reader should continue for all twelve major keys. Diatonic seventh chords for all keys are listed in the Appendix. (p. 140.) A knowledge of diatonic seventh chords in all keys is indispensable for playing jazz. By mastering these basic exercises, one can easily grasp the relationships among chords within any major key and the relationships among all major keys themselves.

1. RIGHT HAND (RH) CHORDS
LEFT HAND (LH) ROOTS

Play the chord in the right hand (RH) and the root of the chord in the left hand (LH). Start on the tonic of the major scale and play each diatonic seventh chord of the scale while ascending to the tonic an octave higher. Continue by playing each diatonic seventh chord while descending back to the original position.

Fig. 1-1

Key of C Major

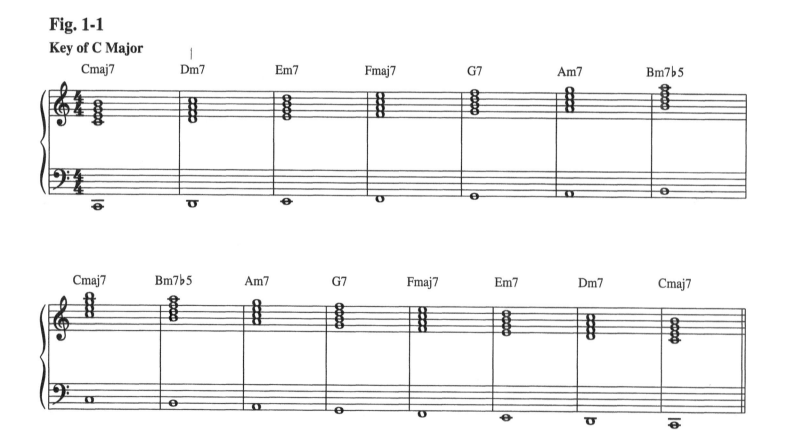

Key of G Major

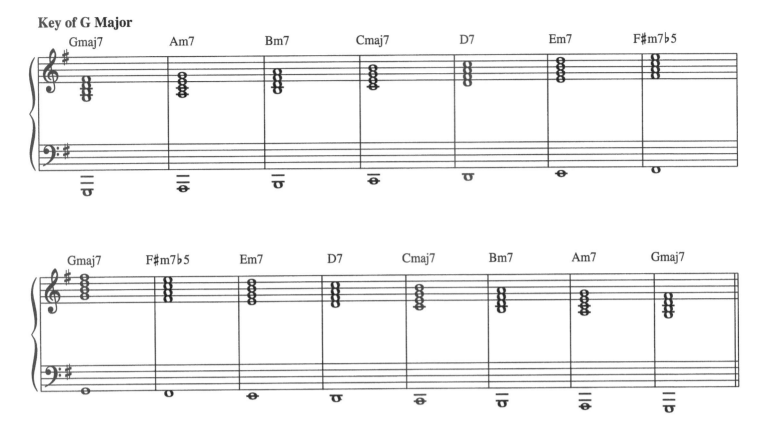

2. LH CHORDS ALONE

Play diatonic seventh chords in the left hand alone. Proceed as before.

Fig. 1-2

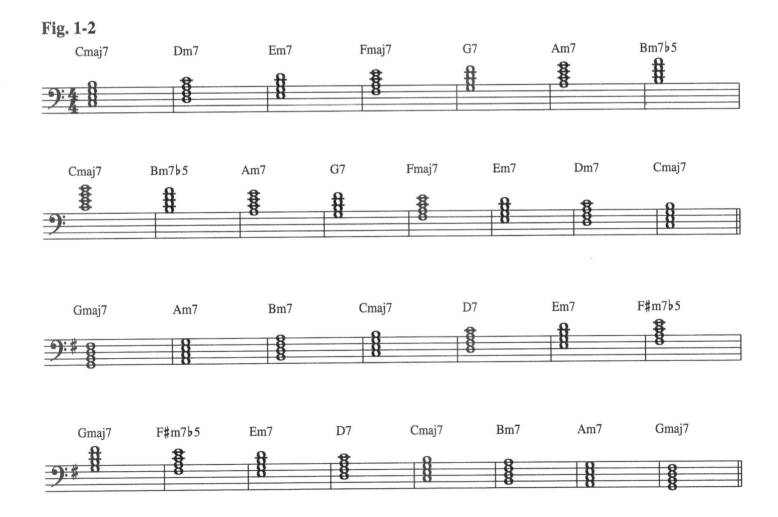

3. RH ASCENDING ARPEGGIOS
LH CHORDS

Play each note of each chord by ascending from the root in the right hand. Play the full chord in the left hand while arpeggiating each chord in the right hand.

Fig. 1-3

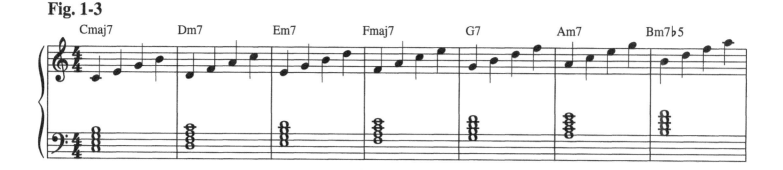

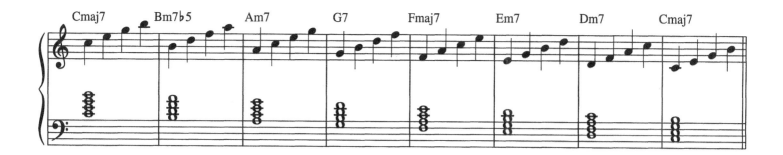

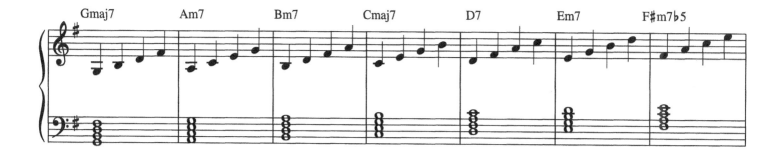

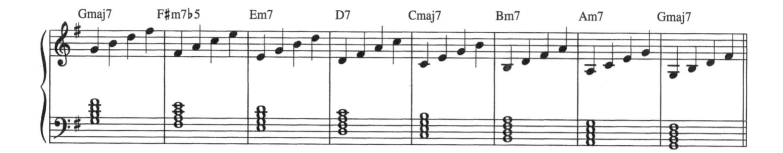

4. RH DESCENDING ARPEGGIOS
LH CHORDS

Play each note of each chord by descending from the seventh in the right hand. Play the full chord in the left hand while arpeggiating each chord in the right hand. Proceed as before.

Fig. 1-4

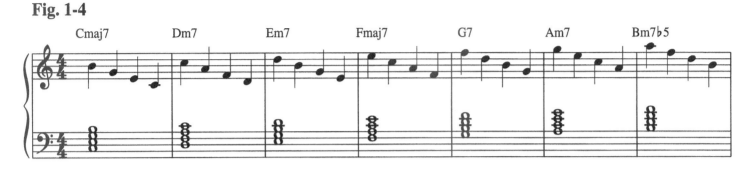

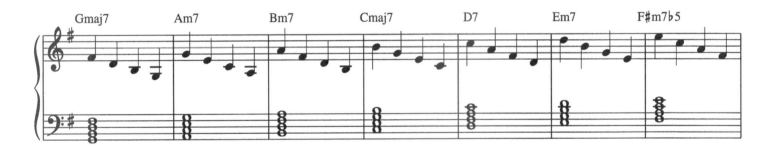

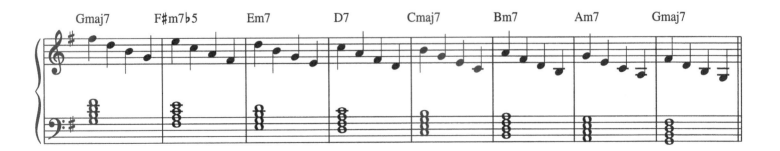

One does not need to master every key before proceeding to the next lesson. Learn all four exercises in several keys now and continue with the remaining keys while working on the next lesson. See Appendix, p. 140.

LESSON 2
II-V-I PROGRESSIONS
MAJOR KEYS
CLOSE POSITION FORMULA 1

A chord progression is a series of chords that connect to each other. Certain chord progressions are used more often than others and these common progressions will be studied to facilitate easy learning and recognition. The most common chord progression used in jazz is the II-V-I progression. Within any particular key, a II chord is followed by a V chord and the V chord is followed by a I chord. Thus, in the key of C major, a II-V-I progression based on seventh chords is Dm7-G7-Cmaj7. The same progression in G major is Am7-D7-Gmaj7. Similar chords for II-V-I progressions can be determined by locating each chord in the diatonic seventh system for each major key. Remember that in major keys, a II chord is always a minor seventh chord, a V chord is always a dominant seventh chord and a I chord is always a major seventh or a major sixth chord.

The relative position of each chord to each other in a II-V-I progression allows one to make each chord change smoother by inverting certain chords. The process of leading each note of one chord into each note of the next chord is called voice leading. II-V-I progressions lend themselves to a simple and effective voice leading formula. By inverting the V chord to a 2nd inversion position and keeping the II and I chords in root position, the movement from chord to chord is kept to a minimum. This will be referred to as Close Position Formula 1 or **CPF1.**

Fig. 2-1

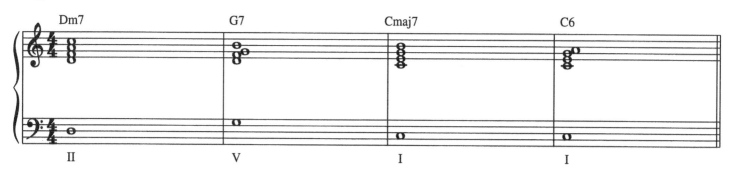

I chords in major keys can be major seventh chords or major sixth chords. The sixth is used freely in jazz as an equivalent or a substitute for a major seventh chord. In the following examples, both the major seventh and major sixth chord will be used as I chords. Thus, there will be two forms of the I chord. In the key of C major, for instance, both Cmaj7 and C6 are used as I chords.

Below is a list of II-V-I progressions for each major key. The chord voicings are in the right hand and the roots of the chords are in the left hand.

Fig. 2-2

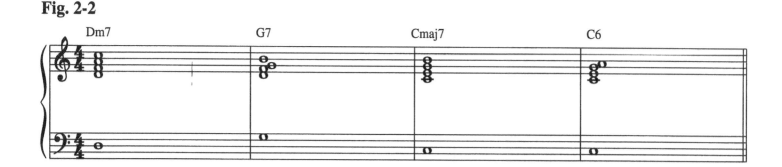

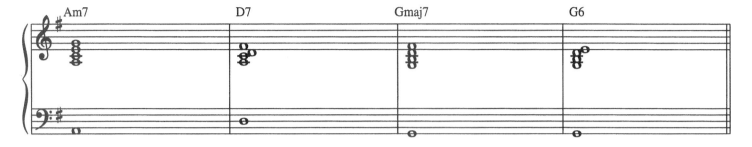

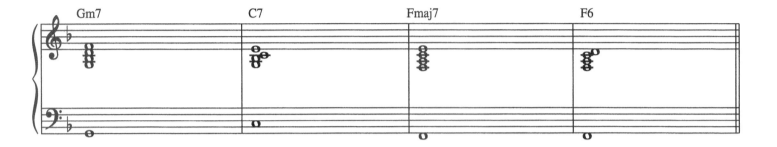

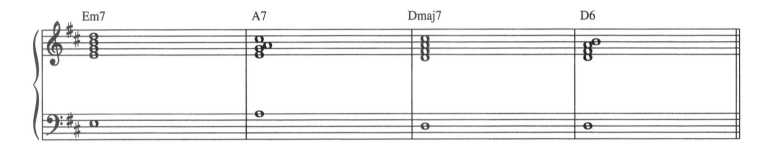

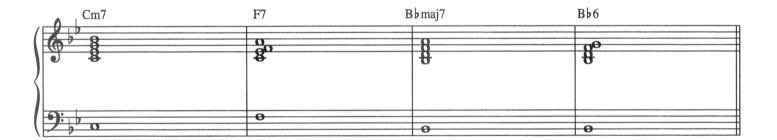

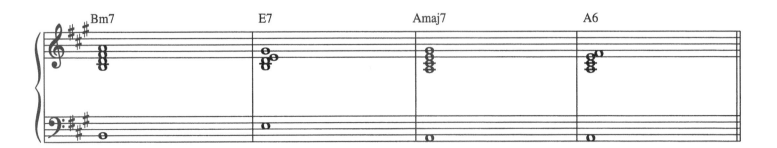

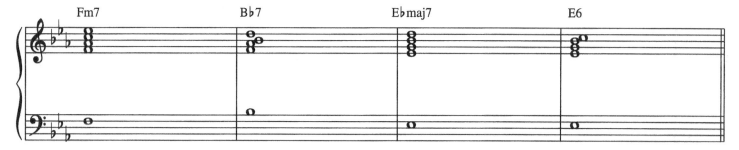

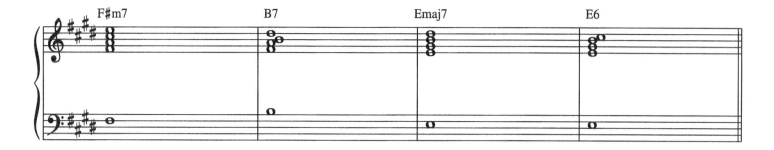

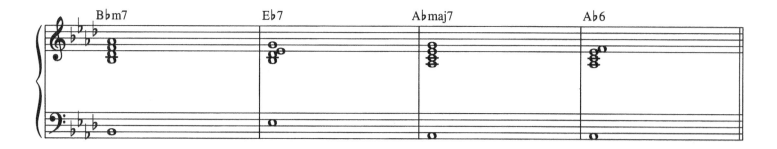

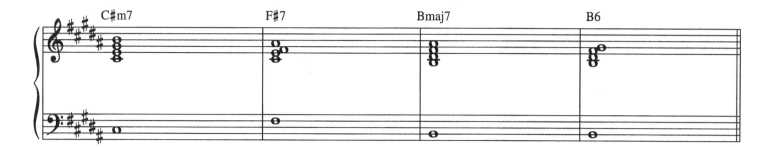

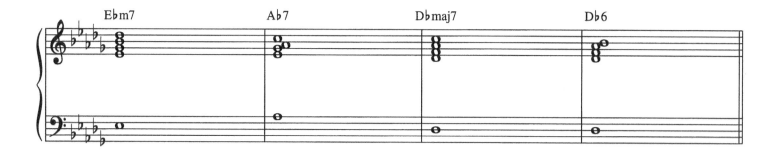

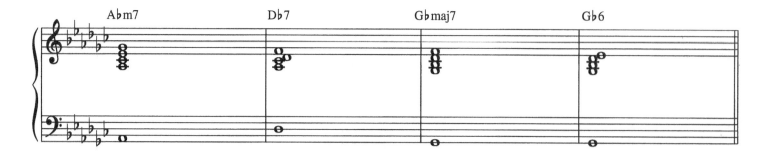

The following exercises represent three ways of practicing the II-V-I Close Position Formula 1 (**CPF1**) for each major key. Practice in all twelve major keys in the same order of keys as the diatonic seventh chord exercises: C, G, F, D, B♭, A, E♭, E, A♭, B, D♭, G♭. The student should master each exercise in each key in the order given before proceeding to the next key. The fingering given is highly recommended and should be the same for each pattern. Examples in the keys of C and G major are given below.

1. RH CHORDS
LH ROOTS

Play the chords in the right hand. Follow the voice leading principles of Close Position Formula 1. Play the root of each chord in the left hand.

Fig. 2-3

Key of C Major

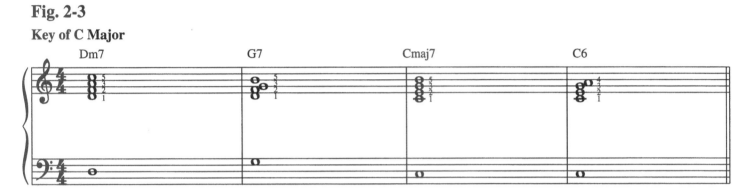

Key of G Major

2. LH CHORDS ALONE

Play the chords in the left hand. Follow the voice leading principles of Close Position Formula 1.

Fig. 2-4

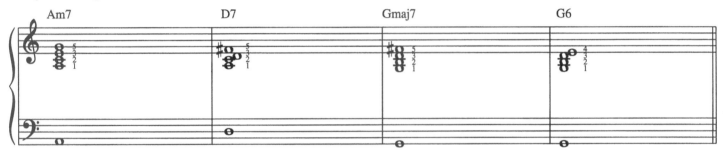

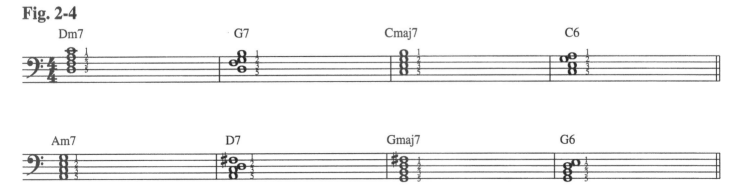

3. RH ARPEGGIOS
LH CHORDS

Alternate ascending and descending arpgeggios for each chord in the right hand. Play the chords in the left hand as before. Observe the fingering for the right hand arpeggios: the fingering is the same as that used for playing the full chords. This is not necessarily a good fingering for these single note motions, but it will reinforce the chord fingering and help to formulate the chord voicings and progressions.

Fig. 2-5

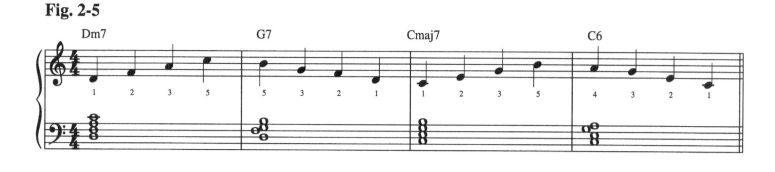

II-V-I PROGRESSIONS IN DESCENDING WHOLE STEPS

II-V-I progressions often follow each other in keys that are a whole step below each other. Playing II-V-I progressions in the order of descending whole steps is a useful exercise in recognizing this pattern and, in general, is a convenient way to practice II-V-I progressions.

Since changing keys in descending whole steps will circle back to the original key after six keys, two separate cycles are necessary. The following order in each cycle should be used: C, Bb, Ab, Gb, E, D, and Eb, Db, B, A, G, F. These cycles may actually start in any desired key.

Play the progressions as in Exercises 1, 2, and 3, but now in the order of two cycles of descending whole steps.

Fig. 2-6

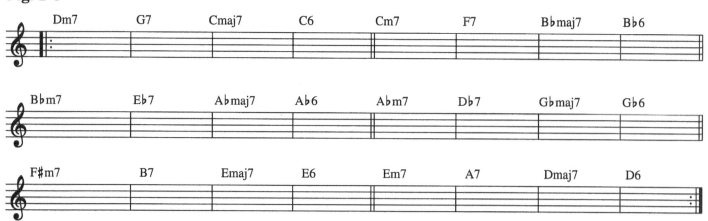

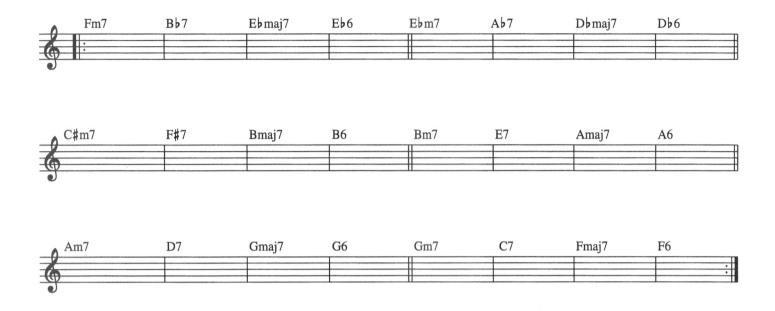

ALTERNATING II-V PROGRESSIONS

Often II-V progressions occur without necessarily going to I chords. Thus, a II-V progression can be succeeded by the same or a different II-V progression without a I chord. Alternating II-V progressions can be practiced easily by proceeding in two cycles of descending whole steps, as shown below. Practice II-V progressions by following the procedures in Exercises 1, 2, and 3 on pages 17 and 18.

Fig. 2-7

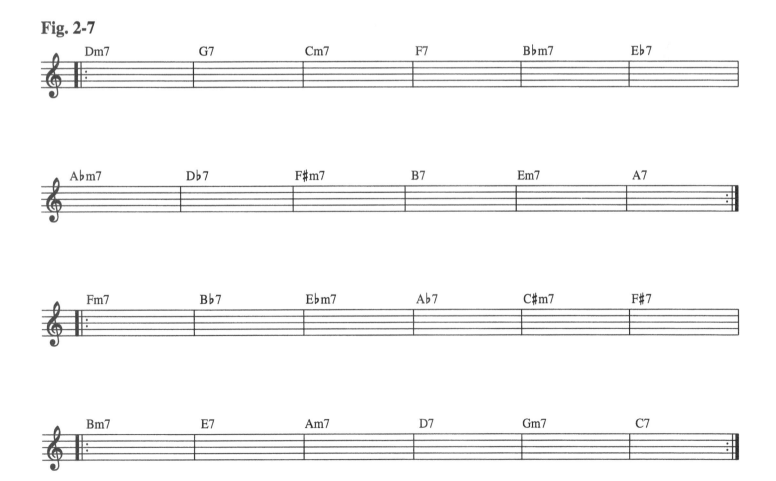

LESSON 3
APPLYING CLOSE POSITION FORMULA 1 - CPF1
MAJOR KEYS

The following music is written in a typical "lead sheet" fashion. It includes a melody and chord symbols. The chord symbols indicate chord progressions that are intended to accompany the melody. It is up to the player to play from a lead sheet in a stylistically appropriate manner. Jazz musicians essentially read a bare outline of a tune and proceed to make music from it. Each individual player may interpret this outline in a unique way and there are many possible solutions for the realization of any lead sheet. Chord voicings, rhythm, feel, and other nuances can vary from player to player, and from performance to performance.

The goal of this lesson is for the player to make the simplest realization possible for this lead sheet. Therefore, strict voicing rules will be observed. As the book progresses, more elaborate possibilities will be offered. The following rules and formulas are presented to establish a firm understanding of the basic chords and chord motions that are used in most jazz situations. Our goal is to be able to play a simple melody and chords from a lead sheet.

LUNAR ECLIPSE

"Lunar Eclipse" is a tune that uses several II-V-I and diatonic seventh chord progressions. Use the following rules when playing "Lunar Eclipse:"

RULES: Play all chords in root position except V chords that are a part of a II-V-I or a II-V progression, in which case apply Close Position Formula 1. **CPF1.** Play these V chords (dominant seventh chords) in second inversion. V chords that are not part of a II-V-I or a II-V progression should be played in root position.

II-V-I and II-V progressions can occur in any key within a tune. The reader must recognize when these progressions occur and use the rule accordingly. Study the chord progressions before playing. Circling the II-V-I and II-V progressions may help the reader to recognize these when they occur. Lead sheets for "Lunar Eclipse" and other tunes in this book are found in the Appendix. See p. 146 for "Lunar Eclipse."

Play "Lunar Eclipse" in the following three ways and in the order presented:

1. RH CHORDS
LH ROOTS

Play just the chord changes (no melody) using the voicing rules above with the right hand and the roots of each chord in the left hand. The example below presents this procedure for the first half of "Lunar Eclipse." Continue for the rest of the tune by referring to the lead sheet.

Fig. 3-1 Lunar Eclipse

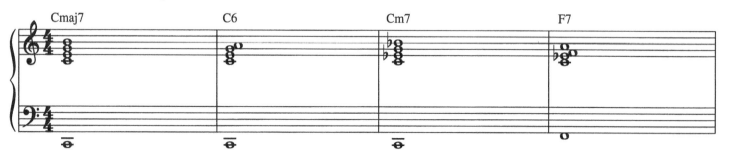

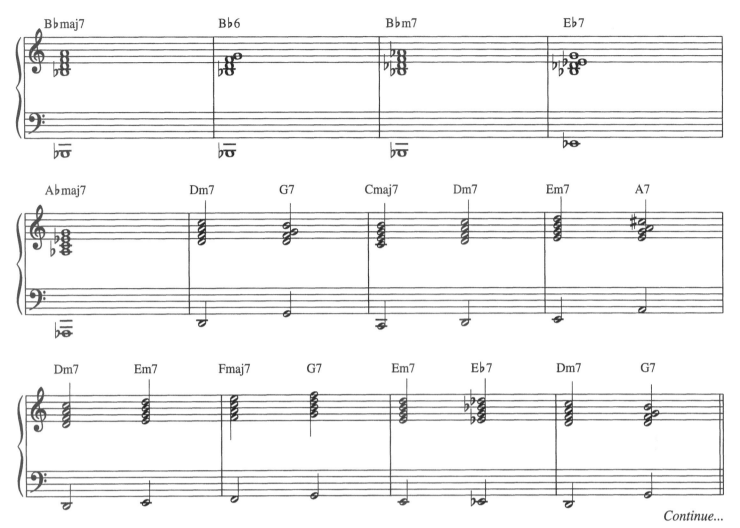

Continue...

2. LH CHORDS ALONE

Play the chords as above but an octave lower with the left hand alone. The example illustrates this procedure for the first half of the tune. Continue as before.

Fig. 3-2 Lunar Eclipse

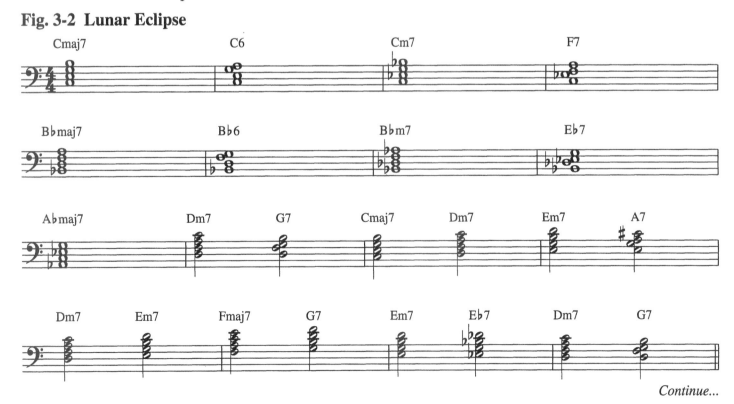

Continue...

3. RH MELODY
LH CHORDS

Play the chords in the left hand as in the previous example and play the melody in single notes in the right hand at the same time. Fig. 3-3 illustrates this procedure for the first half of the tune.

Fig. 3-3 Lunar Eclipse

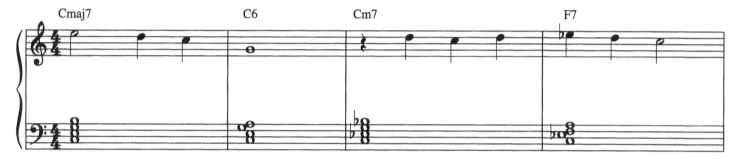

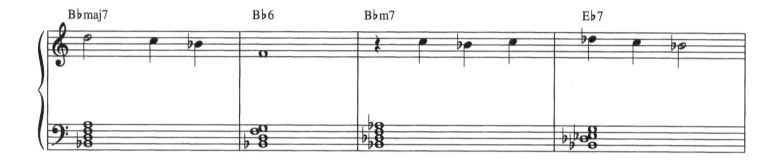

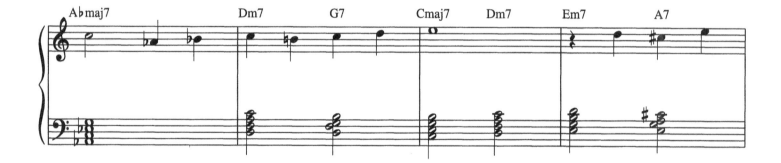

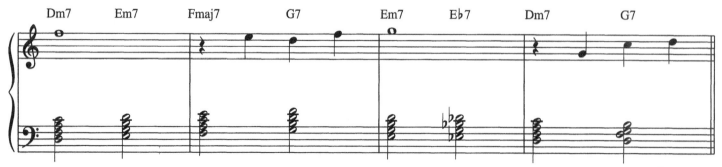

Continue...

LESSON 4

II-V-I PROGRESSIONS
MINOR KEYS
CLOSE POSITION FORMULA 1

There are essentially three different minor scales used in tonal music, as opposed to just one major scale. Minor keys, then, are more problematic than major keys. Since there are different scales used in minor keys, diatonic seventh chords in minor do not fit so neatly as they do in major. Because of this, diatonic seventh chords in minor will not be systematically practiced as they were in major. (See the Introduction for more information on minor keys).

Although the minor mode is more complex and ambiguous than the major mode, there are certain parallels. A relationship among chords exists and certain chord progressions are common. II-V-I progressions in minor are often used and they function in a similar way to II-V-I progressions in major. In minor, a II chord is a minor seventh flat five chord - m7♭5, (sometimes referred to as a half-diminished seventh chord, ∅7) a V chord is a dominant seventh chord (the same as in major), and a I chord can be a minor-major seventh chord - m(maj7) or a minor sixth chord - m6.

The following is a II-V-I progression in C minor.

Fig. 4-1

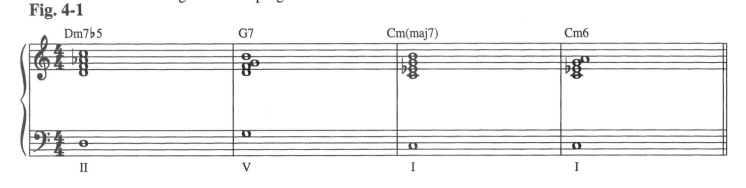

The example below lists II-V-I progressions for each minor key. These are listed in a similar way to the major II-V-I progressions presented in Lesson 2.

Fig. 4-2

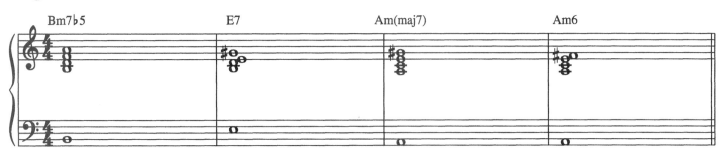

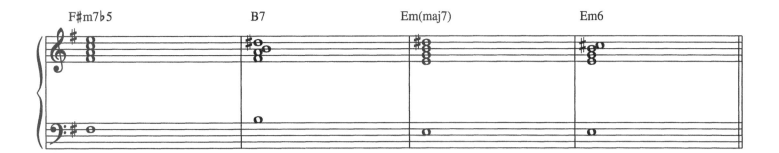

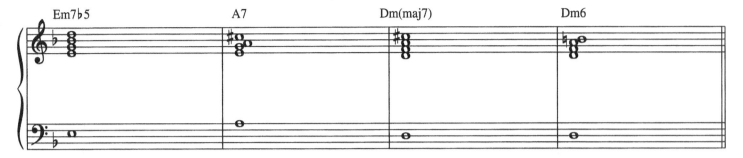

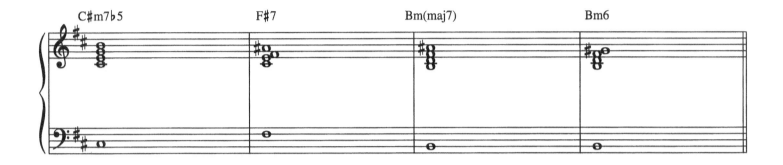

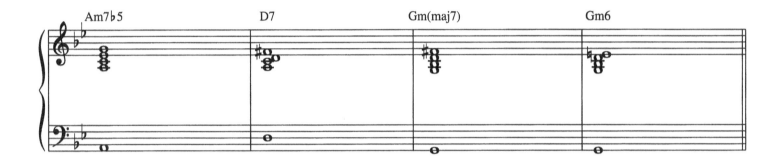

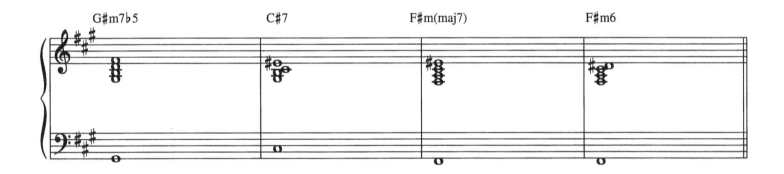

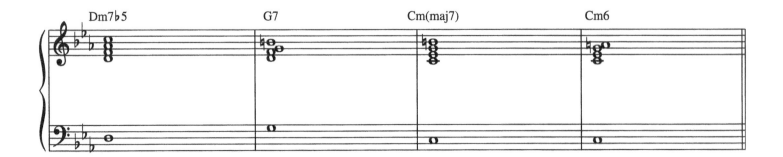

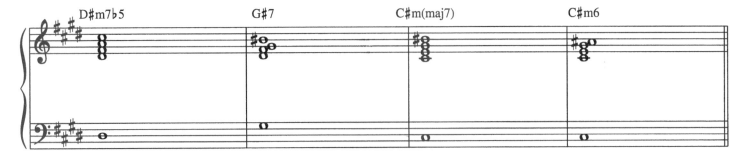

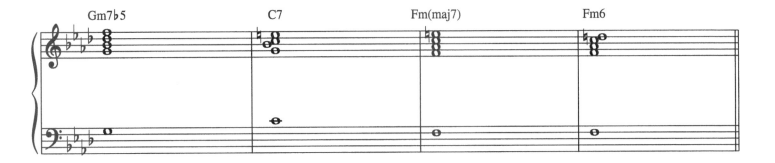

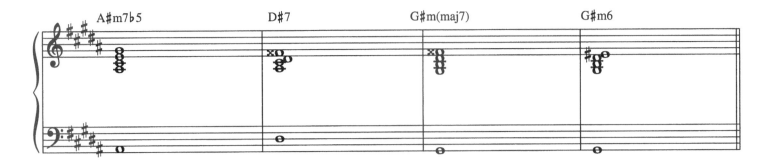

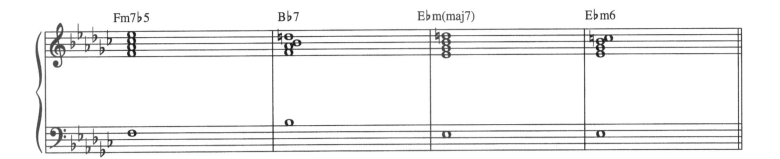

The following exercises present three ways of practicing the II-V-I Close Position Formula 1 for each minor key. Practice in all twelve minor keys. Practice in the order of increasing sharps and flats as follows: Am, Em, Dm, Bm Gm, F#m, Cm, C#m, Fm, G#m, Bbm, Ebm. Practice and master each exercise in each key in the order given before proceeding to the next key. Use the same fingering as for the major keys. Examples in the keys of A and E minor are given below.

II-V-I progressions in minor should be practiced as they were in major.

1. RH CHORDS
LH ROOTS

Play the chords in the right hand following the voice leading principles of Close Position Formula 1. Play the root of each chord in the left hand.

Fig. 4-3

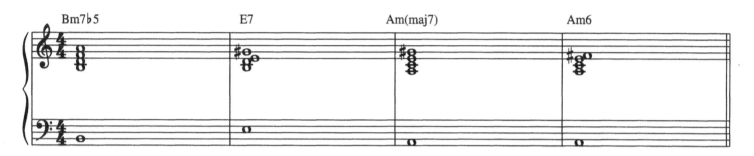

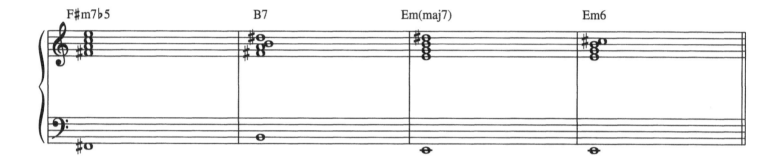

2. LH CHORDS

Play the chords in the left hand and follow the voice leading principles of Close Position Formula 1.

Fig. 4-4

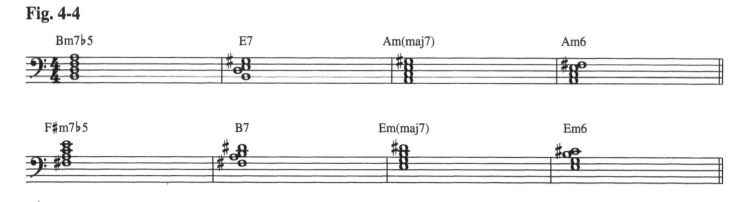

3. RH ARPEGGIOS
LH CHORDS

Alternate ascending and descending arpeggios for each chord in the right hand. Play the chords in the left hand as before. Observe the fingering for the right hand arpeggios. The fingering is the same as that for playing the full chords. This is not necessarily a good fingering for these single note motions, but it will reinforce the chord fingering and help to formulate the chord voicings and progressions.

Fig. 4-5

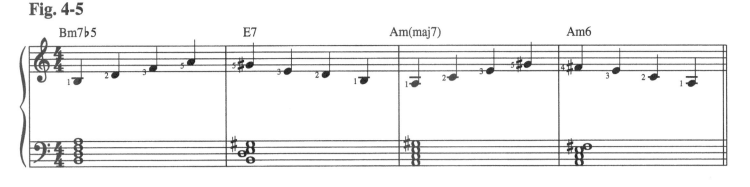

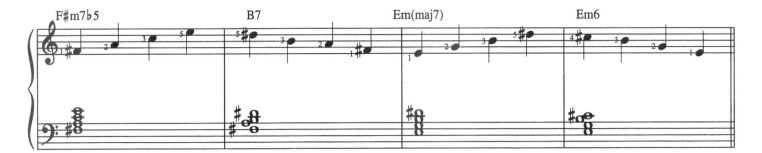

II-V-I PROGRESSIONS IN DESCENDING WHOLE STEPS

Play the progressions as in exercises 1, 2, and 3, but now in the order of two cycles of descending whole steps (see Lesson 2). Use the following two cycles of keys: Am, Gm Fm, Ebm, C#m, Bm and Cm, Bbm, G#m, F#m, Em, Dm.

Fig. 4-6

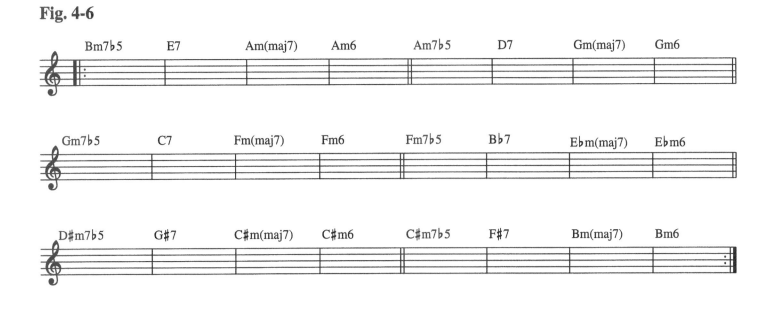

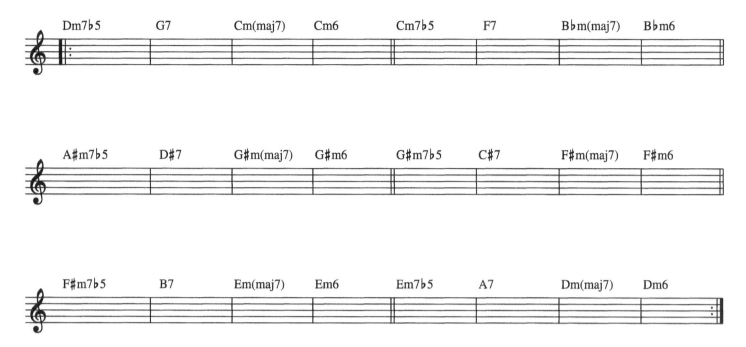

| Dm7b5 | G7 | Cm(maj7) | Cm6 | Cm7b5 | F7 | Bbm(maj7) | Bbm6 |

| A#m7b5 | D#7 | G#m(maj7) | G#m6 | G#m7b5 | C#7 | F#m(maj7) | F#m6 |

| F#m7b5 | B7 | Em(maj7) | Em6 | Em7b5 | A7 | Dm(maj7) | Dm6 |

ALTERNATING II-V PROGRESSIONS

Often II-V progressions occur without necessarily going to I chords. Thus, a II-V progression can be succeeded by the same or a different II-V progression without a I chord. Alternating II-V progressions can be practiced easily by proceeding in two cycles of descending whole steps. Practice II-V progressions (without I chords) by following the procedures in Exercises 1, 2, and 3.

Fig. 4-7

| Bm7b5 | E7 | Am7b5 | D7 | Gm7b5 | C7 |

| Fm7b5 | Bb7 | Ebm7b5 | Ab7 | C#m7b5 | F#7 |

| Dm7b5 | G7 | Cm7b5 | F7 | Bbm7b5 | Eb7 |

| Abm7b5 | Db7 | F#m7b5 | B7 | Em7b5 | A7 |

LESSON 5

APPLYING CLOSE POSITION FORMULA 1
MINOR KEYS

Within the context of any tune, II-V-I progressions can occur in several major and minor keys. Major and minor modes are often mixed within a single progression. For instance, a II-V major progression can proceed to a minor I chord, and a II-V minor progression can proceed to a major I chord.

Fig. 5-1

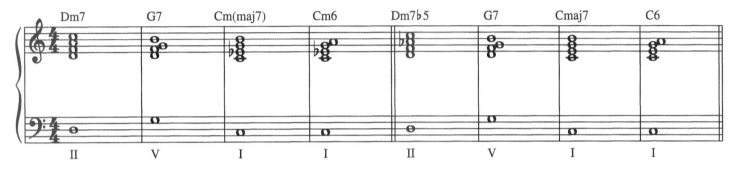

MINORS ALLOWED

"Minors Allowed" is a tune in A minor that also moves to other keys. There are minor, major, and mixed II-V-I progressions as well as II-V progressions. Follow the same rules and procedures as for "Lunar Eclipse" (see Lesson 3). See p. 144 of the Appendix for the lead sheet.

RULES: Play all chords in root position except V chords that are a part of a II-V-I or a II-V progression (major or minor). In these cases, Close Position Formula 1 will apply. Play these V chords (dominant seventh chords) in second inversion. V chords that are not part of a II-V-I or a II-V progression should be played in root position.

Play "Minors Allowed" in the same ways as "Lunar Eclipse."

1. RH CHORDS
LH ROOTS

Fig. 5-2 Minors Allowed

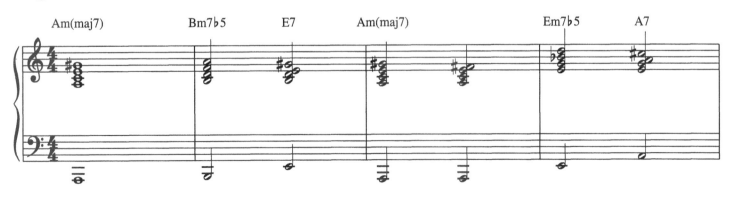

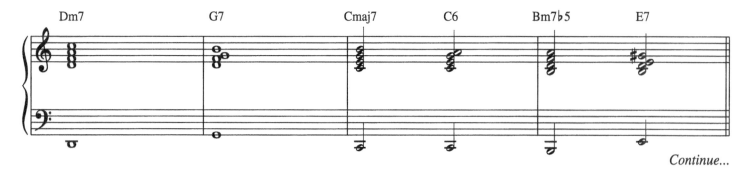

Continue...

2. LH CHORDS ALONE

Fig. 5-3 Minors Allowed

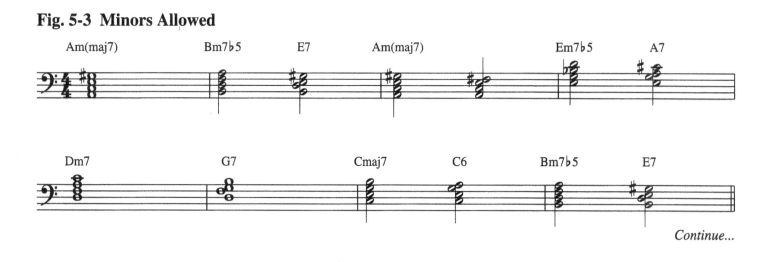

Continue...

3. RH MELODY
LH CHORDS

Fig. 5-4 Minors Allowed

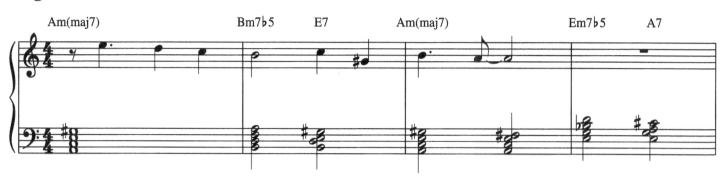

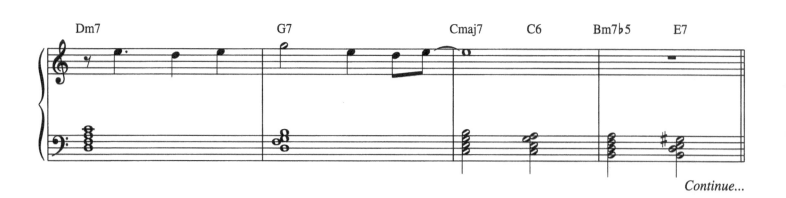

Continue...

LESSON 6
CIRCLE OF FIFTHS PROGRESSIONS
AND ROOT MOVEMENT BY FIFTH

Close Position Formula 1 works the way it does because the roots of each succeeding chord moves down by a fifth. The roots of the chords in a II-V-I progression are a descending fifth apart. In the Key of C major, a II-V-I progression is Dm7-G7-Cmaj7. G is a fifth lower than D, and C is a fifth lower than G. When roots move down by a fifth, root position chords easily alternate with second inversion chords as demonstrated in **CPF1.** The most common root movement in tonal music is by descending fifths, and progressions other than II-V-I and II-V progressions are common.

Below is what is known as the Circle of Fifths. All twelve possible roots are arranged clockwise in descending fifths around a circle to represent all fifth relationships.

Fig. 6-1

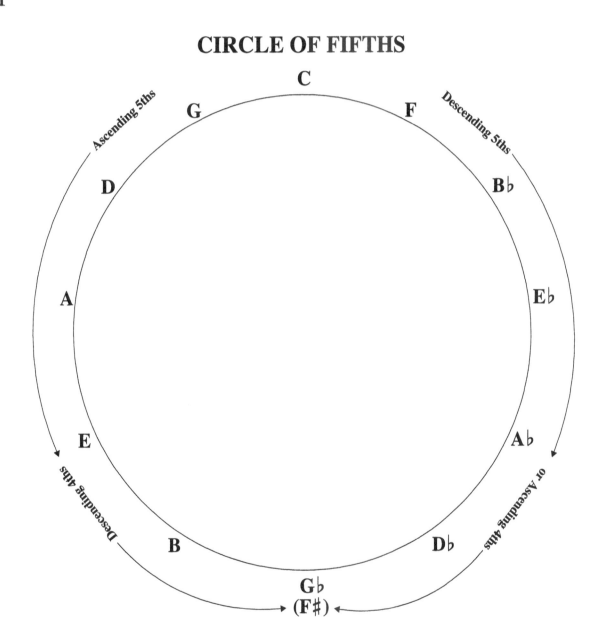

The motion can be reversed to counter-clockwise and the circle can be thought of as ascending fifths or descending fourths.

Although root movement down by a fifth is common, the chord qualities and types of progressions can vary greatly. There are many types of descending fifth progressions and the number of chords that can be involved can vary from two to many. The II-V-I progressions in major and minor are just two possibilities.

The following exercises represent circle of fifths progressions that isolate a particular chord quality. Root position chords will alternate with second inversion chords. Two cycles are presented for each exercise in order to accommodate all possible combinations.

I-IV PROGRESSIONS-MAJOR 7TH CHORD MOVEMENT

This exercise illustrates a series of major seventh chords moving around the circle of fifths. Often, this type of movement occurs during a I-IV progression in major. In F major the I chord, Fmaj7, often moves to a Bbmaj7 chord. Although Bbmaj7 is the IV chord, its root is a fifth lower (as well as a 4th higher) than F. This relationship can be extended to the next chord in the cycle, Ebmaj7, which is the IV chord in Bb major. The entire cycle of major seventh chords can be viewed as overlapping I-IV progressions in major.

Practice this exercise in two ways.

1. RH CHORDS
LH ROOTS

Fig. 6-2

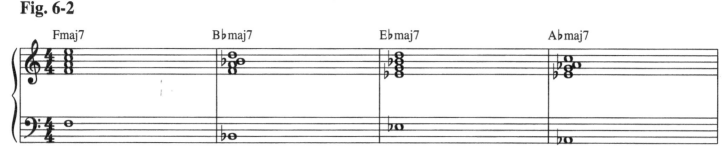

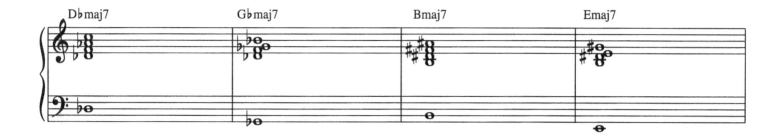

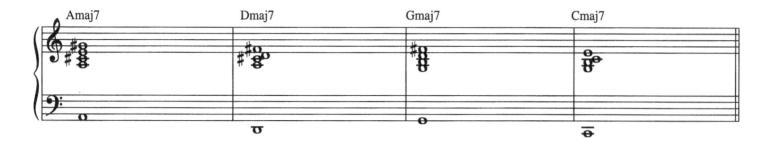

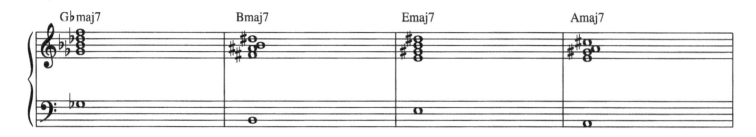

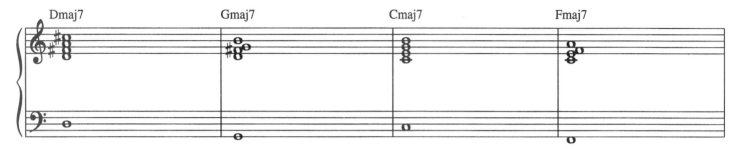

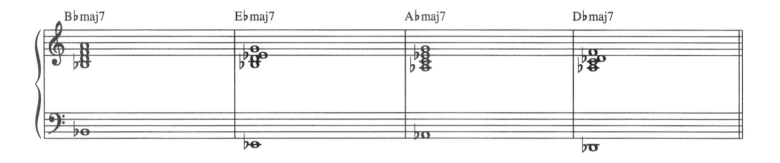

2. LH CHORDS

Fig. 6-3

III-VI PROGRESSIONS-MINOR 7TH CHORD MOVEMENT

This exercise illustrates a series of minor seventh chords moving around the circle of fifths. This type of movement often occurs during a III-VI progression in major. In C major the III chord, Em7, often moves to an Am7, the VI chord. This relationship can be extended through all the major keys by playing minor seventh chords around the circle of fifths. An Am7 can be the III chord in F major which can move to the VI chord, Dm7, and so on.

1. RH CHORDS
LH ROOTS

Fig. 6-4

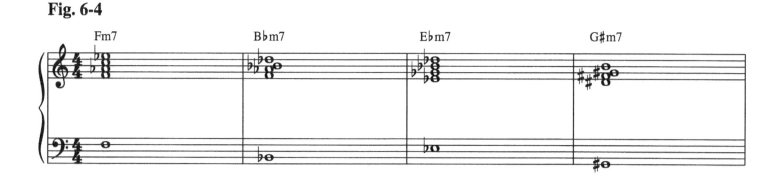

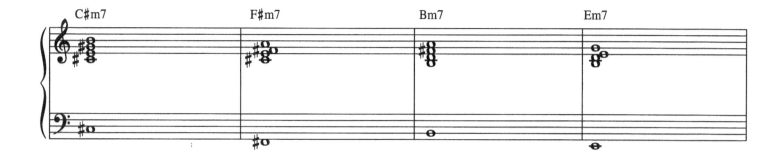

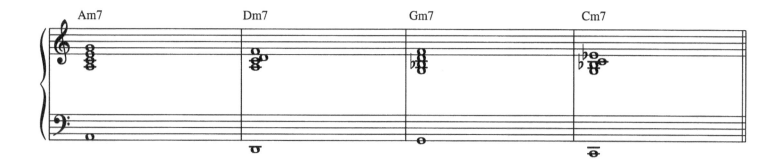

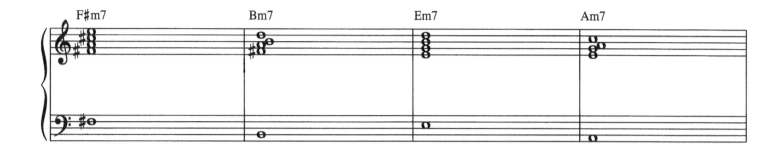

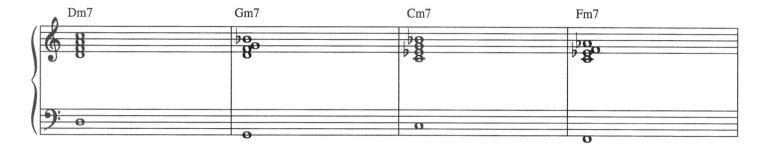

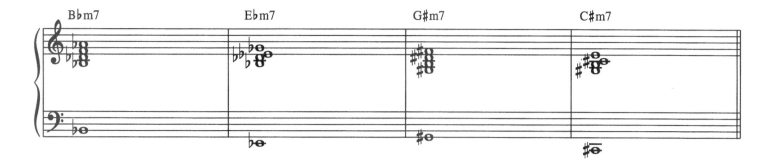

2. LH CHORDS

Fig. 6-5

V of V PROGRESSIONS-DOMINANT 7TH CHORD MOVEMENT

Fig. 6-6 illustrates a series of dominant seventh chords moving around the circle of fifths. Often, this type of movement occurs during a V of V progression. Instead of resolving to I chords, V chords often move to another V chord a 5th lower. Thus, the first V chord has become a V chord of another V chord. For example, G7, the V chord in C major can move to C7, the V chord in F major, which then can move to F7, the V chord in B♭ major, and so on. This type of progression is common during sections that change keys quickly. Long chains of dominant seventh chords moving around the circle of fifths are common.

1. RH CHORDS
LH ROOTS

Fig. 6-6

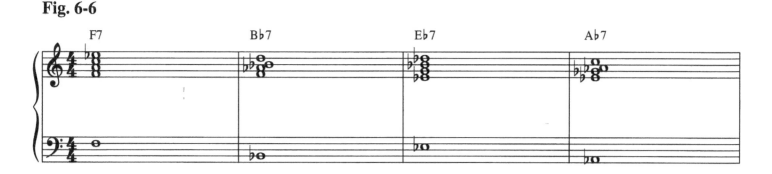

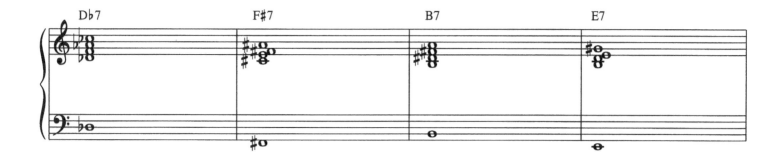

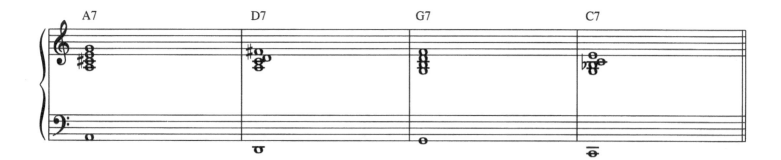

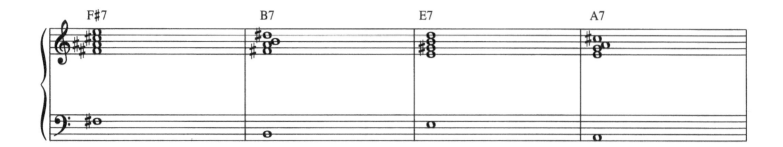

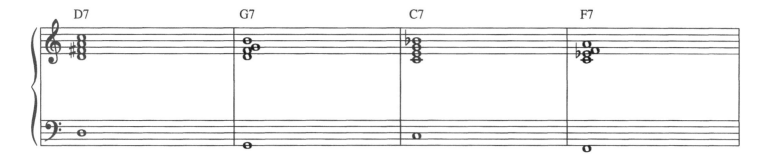

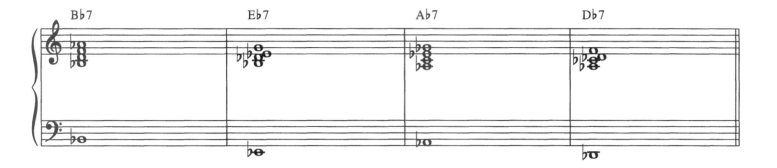

2. LH CHORDS

Fig. 6-7

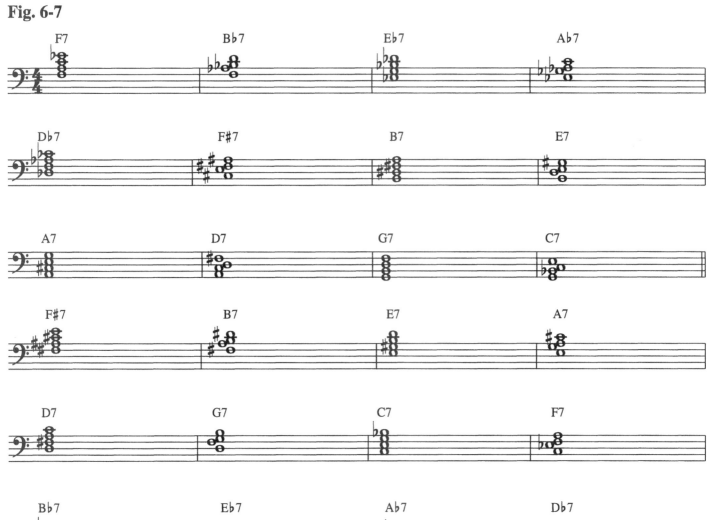

AUTUMN WONDERLAND

"Autumn Wonderland" makes use of all of the preceding progressions. I-IV, III-VI, and V of V progressions as well as II-V-I and II-V are employed. See p. 149 of the Appendix for the lead sheet. The first eight measures present a II-V-I progression in C major and A minor separated by a "pivot chord," Fmaj7. A pivot chord is one that functions in two different keys at the same time. The Fmaj7 functions as a IV chord in C major and as a VI chord in A minor. The entire cycle of chords during the first eight measures moves down the circle of 5ths from D to A: D-G-C-F-B-E-A. The interval between F and B is not a perfect fifth but a diminished fifth. This does not interrupt the circle of fifths movement.

Notice the I-IV relationship in measures 3-4 and 19-20; the III-VI relationship in measures 11-12, and the V of V relationships in measures 25-28.

An extension to Close Position Formula 1 can be made by alternating root position chords with second inversion chords as long as the chords move down the circle of fifths.

Play "Autumn Wonderland" by starting each eight measure section with a root position chord. Alternate second inversion chords with root position chords when each succeeding root moves down by a 5th. It is sometimes important to break the alternating root position to second inversion routine - as in measure 9 - in order to keep the chord voicings in an appropriate register.

Play "Autumn Wonderland" in the following ways:

1. RH CHORDS
LH ROOTS

Fig. 6-8 Autumn Wonderland

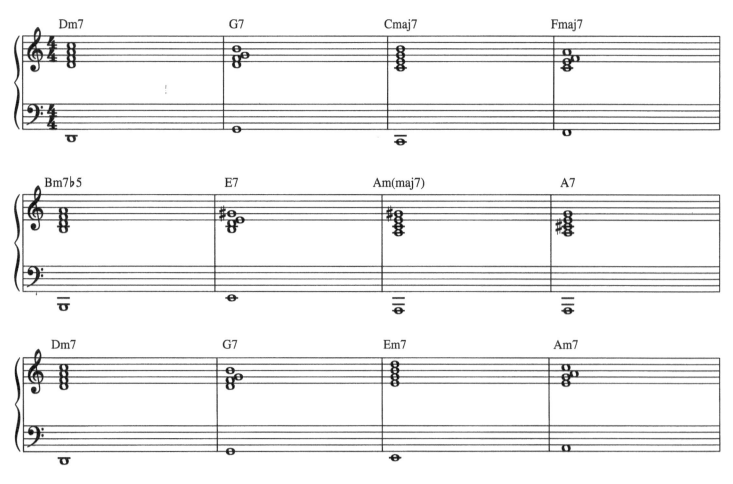

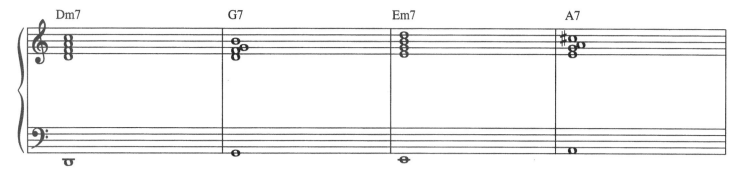

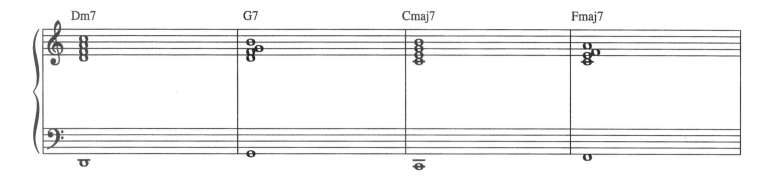

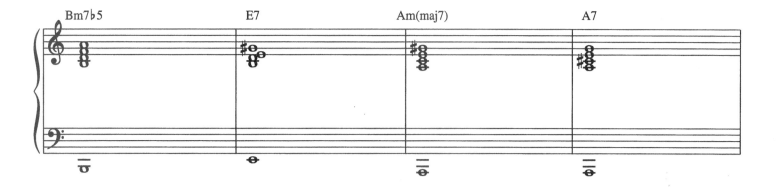

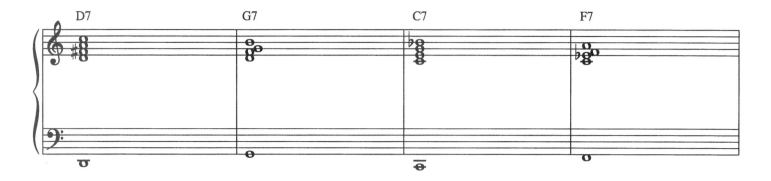

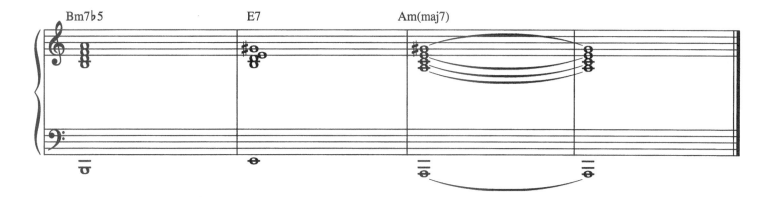

2. LH CHORDS ALONE

Fig. 6-9 Autumn Wonderland

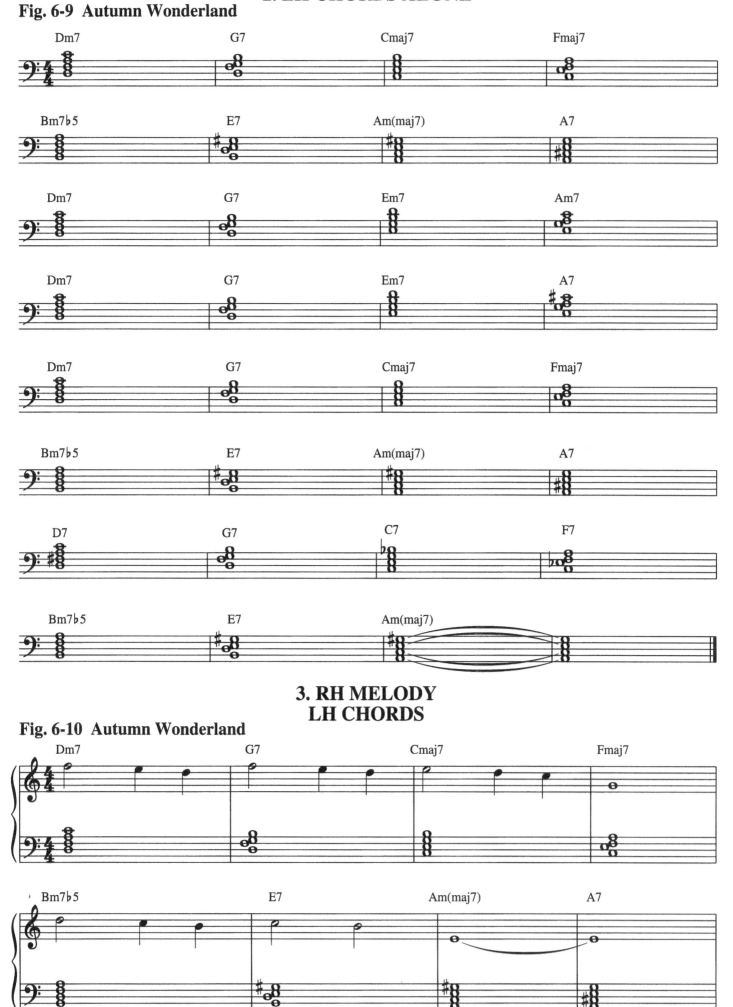

3. RH MELODY
LH CHORDS

Fig. 6-10 Autumn Wonderland

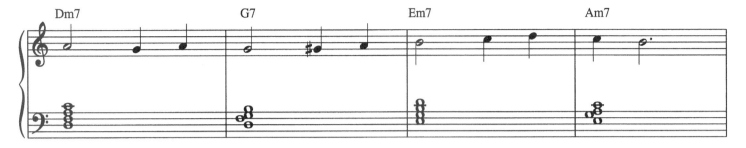

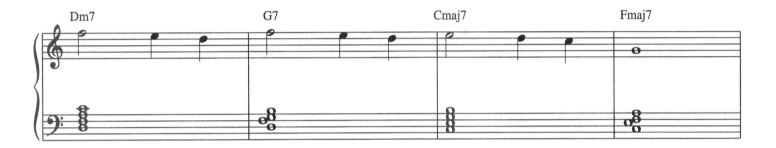

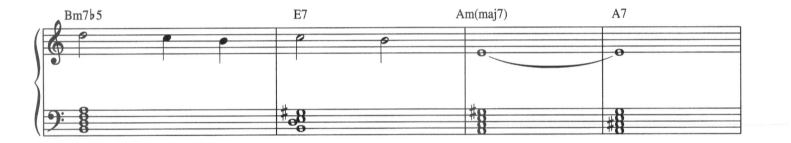

LESSON 7
APPLYING CLOSE POSITION FORMULA 1
SWING FEEL

Jazz is often based on a "swing feel." One way to achieve a swing feel is to play eighth notes unevenly. For a swing feel, the second eighth note in a pair of eighths is played a little after it would be in non-swing music. What is written as two eighth notes is played as a quarter note and eighth note as part of an eighth note triplet. Thus, what is written as ♫ is generally played as ♩³♪. Often one sees ♫ = ♩³♪ at the beginning of written music to indicate swing eighths. Eighth rests are also included in this practice. Tempo and personal preference play an important part in determining exactly how swing eighth notes are played. The faster the tempo, the more evenly they are played. When playing jazz swing styles, one can infer the use of swing eighth notes whether indicated or not. Other jazz styles such as Latin and rock usually use "straight" eighth notes.

SPRING SWING

Play "Spring Swing" using swing eighth notes. Play it in the same three ways as "Lunar Eclipse" and "Autumn Wonderland." (see Lesson 3 and 5). Apply **CPF1** as before for voicing chords. Continue the examples given below. See p. 147 of the Appendix for the lead sheet.

1. RH CHORDS
LH ROOTS

Fig. 7-1 Spring Swing

3. RH MELODY (SWING EIGHTH NOTES)
LH CHORDS

When swing eighth notes are used, the rhythmic principles apply for rests as well as notes. Thus, an eighth note preceded by an eighth rest within a beat is played in the same place as it would if preceded by an eighth note. "Spring Swing" has several examples of this concept. Play all chords on beats one or three as before.

Fig. 7-3 Spring Swing

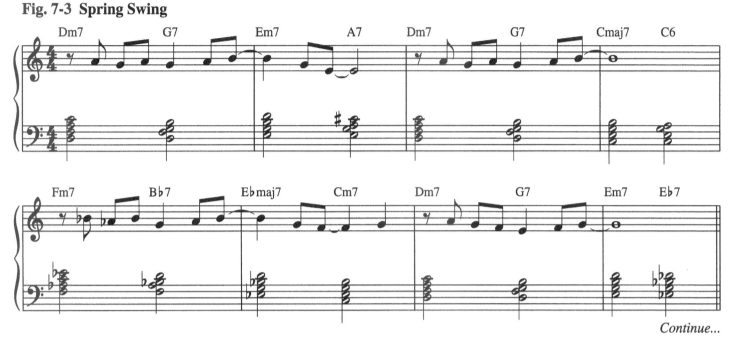

Continue...

An element of swing can be added to the left hand part by separating the root from the rest of the chord in certain places. This works effectively in "Spring Swing" if the following rule is applied:

RULE: If the first melody note of any measure follows an eighth rest on the first beat, play the root of the chord on the first beat and the upper notes (3rd, 5th, 7th) on the following eighth note.

4. RH MELODY
LH CHORDS

Play as in Fig.7-3 but add the new rule to the left hand part.

Fig. 7-4 Spring Swing

Continue...

Jazz musicians often interpret a written melody by changing the rhythms of the melody and by imposing a swing feel on the music. Below are a few samples of how this might be done for tunes already learned. In general, many melody notes that are written and were played on the beat are now placed off the beat, either by pushing the note an eighth note (half of a beat) ahead or behind what is written. Chords can be delayed and anticipated in many different ways.

LUNAR ECLIPSE

Below is a sample of how "Lunar Eclipse" might be played with a swing feel. Notice that both hands rarely play at the same time. When the right hand rests or holds a note, the left hand plays and vice versa. This adds more rhythmic activity and interest than does playing with both hands at the same time. The composite rhythm - the combined rhythm of both hands - helps make the music swing. Remember to apply swing eighth notes to the parts in both hands and to eighth rests as well.

Play through the example and continue in a similar fashion on your own. Also try a version using different rhythms in both hands.

Fig. 7-5. Lunar Eclipse (swing version)

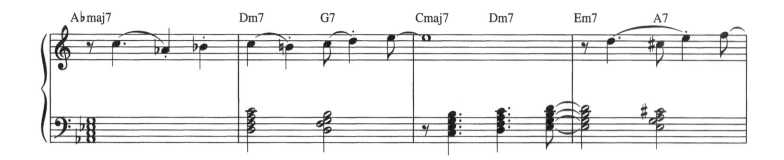

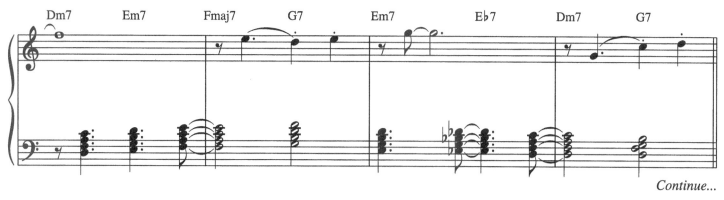

Continue...

MINORS ALLOWED

Below is a sample of how "Minors Allowed" might be played with a swing feel. Notice the similarity to the rhythmic manipulations done to "Lunar Eclipse."

Play through the example and experiment on your own. Try using different rhythms in both hands.

Fig. 7-6

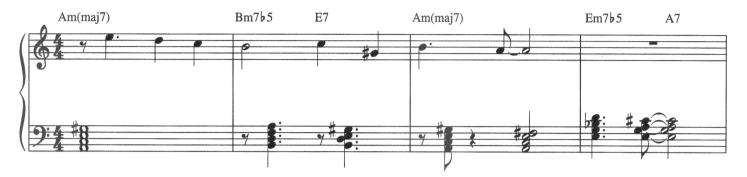

Continue...

AUTUMN WONDERLAND

Invent different swing versions for "Autumn Wonderland." See p. 149 of the Appendix for the lead sheet.

LESSON 8
BASIC STRIDE STYLE

Stride piano refers to a left hand action when a bass note alternates with a chord in a fairly steady quarter-note rhythm. This lesson will present a simple stride approach to playing slow tempo tunes.

SUNNY AND SOUL

"Sunny and Soul" is a medium-slow ballad that should be played with a gentle swing feel. See p. 150 of the Appendix for the lead sheet. Use the following rules:

1. RH MELODY
LH CHORDS IN STRIDE STYLE

RULES: When the duration of a chord is two beats long, play the root of the chord on the first beat and the remaining three notes on the second beat. This essentially splits the root from the rest of a root position chord.

Fig. 8-1

When the duration of a chord is four beats long, play the root of the chord on the first beat and the remaining three notes on the second beat; play the fifth of the chord on the thrid beat and the upper three notes (the same as on the second beat) on the fourth beat.

Fig. 8-2

This rule also applies when there are two different chords of two beats duration within one measure and both chords have the same root.

Fig. 8-3

When a chord lasts for only one beat, play close position chords and apply **CPF1** when appropriate.

Fig. 8-4

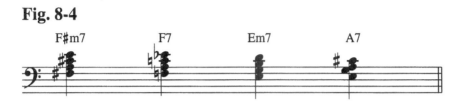

The following example illustrates the first eight measures of "Sunny and Soul."

Fig. 8-5 Sunny and Soul

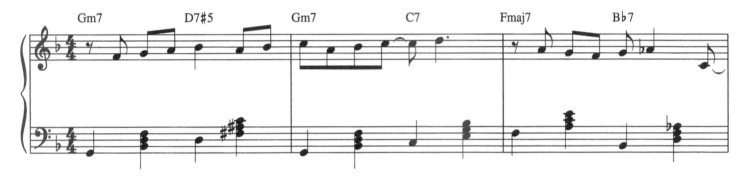

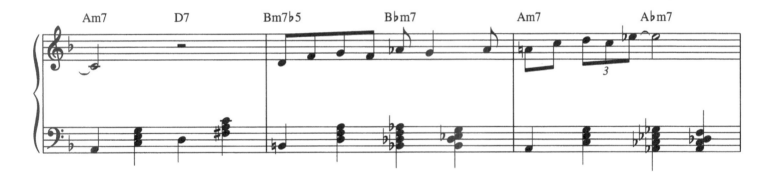

Continue...

LESSON 9
CLOSE POSITION FORMULA 2

II-V-I progressions can be played by reversing the process found in Close Position Formula 1. In Close Position Formula 2 (**CPF2**), the II and I chords are played in second inversion while the V chord is played in root position. Both major and minor keys can be played in **CPF2.**

Fig. 9-1

The following example lists **CPF2** for all twelve major keys.

Fig. 9-2

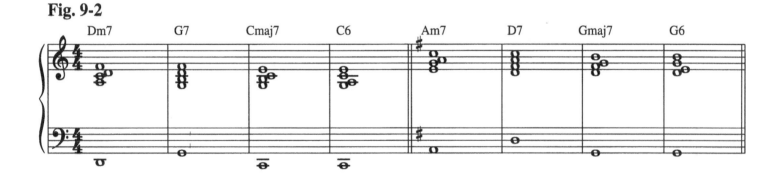

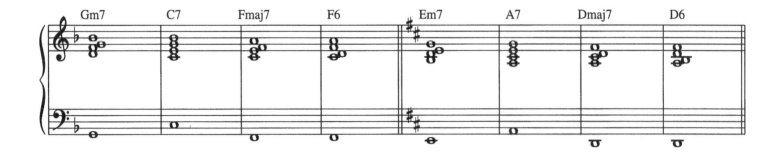

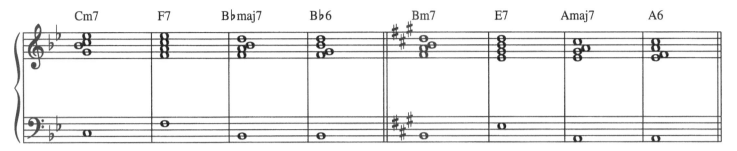

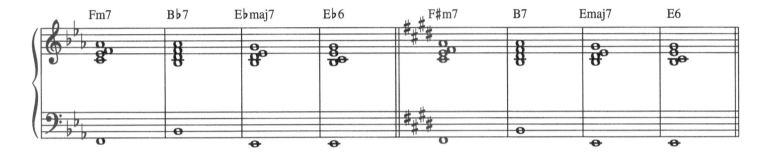

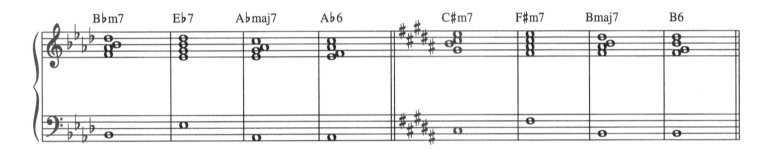

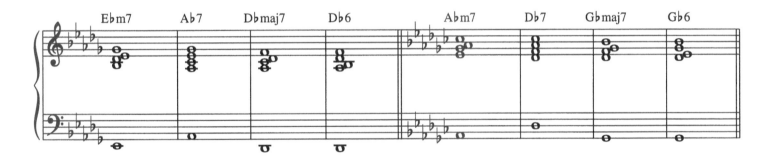

The following example lists **CPF2** for all twelve minor keys.

Fig. 9-3

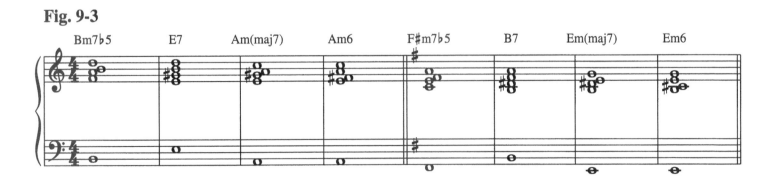

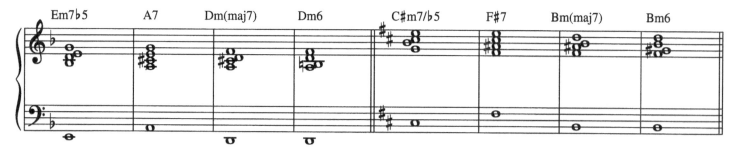

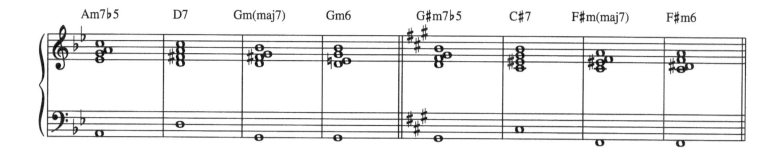

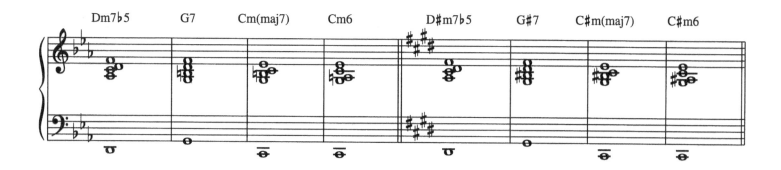

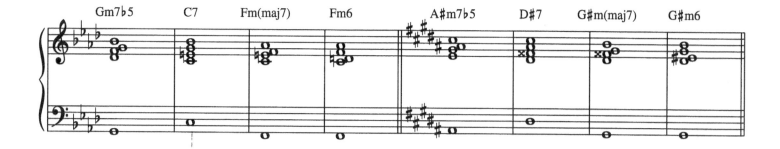

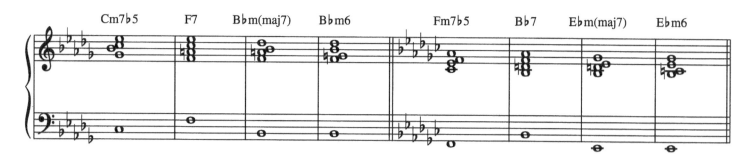

Practice **CPF2** in the same ways as **CPF1** (see Lesson 2). 1. RH chords, LH Roots 2. LH chords alone 3. RH arpeggios, LH chords

LESSON 10
APPLYING CLOSE POSITION FORMULA 2
AND CHORD MELODY

Close Position Formual 2 can be applied in a manner similar to **CPF1.** The following tune offers an opportunity to do so. See p. 148 of the Appendix for the lead sheet.

ALL THE MOON AND THINGS

Play "All the Moon and Things" in the following ways:

1. RH CHORDS
LH ROOTS

Apply **CPF2** to all II-V-I progressions. Play all other chords in root position. The first chord in this tune, Gm7, is not a II chord in this context. It functions as a VI chord in B♭ major. The next minor seventh chord, Cm7, does function as a II chord in B♭ major and is the start of a II-V-I progression. Sections A, B, and D of this tune start in a similar way and all three of these sections are based on a Circle of Fifths Progression. The principle of alternating root position with second inversion chords applies in this context as it did in "Autumn Wonderland" in Lesson 6. Begin Sections A, B, and D with a root position chord.

Fig. 10-1

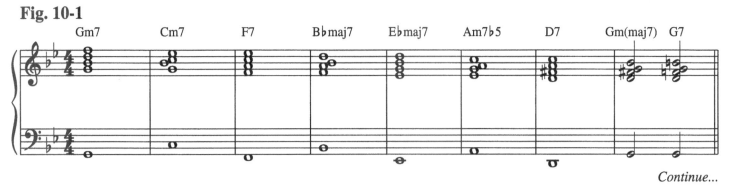

Continue...

Begin section C with a second inversion chord and apply **CPF2** throughout.

Fig. 10-2

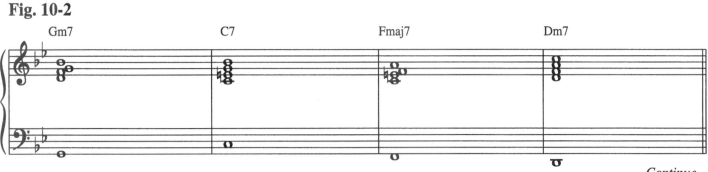

Continue...

2. LH CHORDS

Fig. 10-3 Play the chords in the left hand alone.

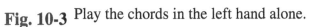

Continue...

3. RH MELODY
LH CHORDS

Play the chords in the left hand and play the melody in single notes in the right hand.

Fig. 10-4 All the Moon and Things

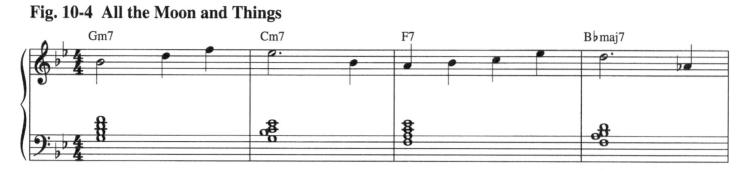

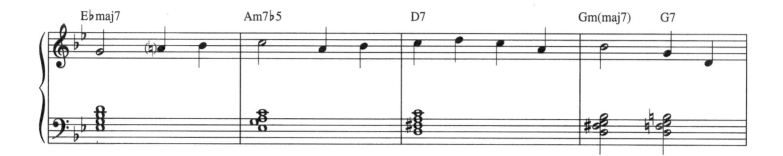

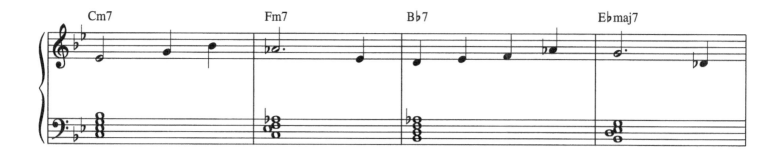

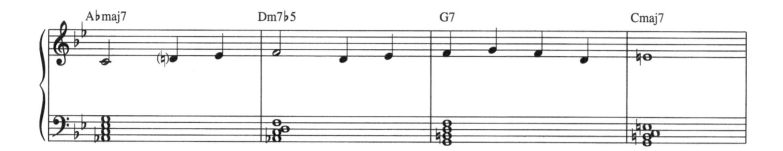

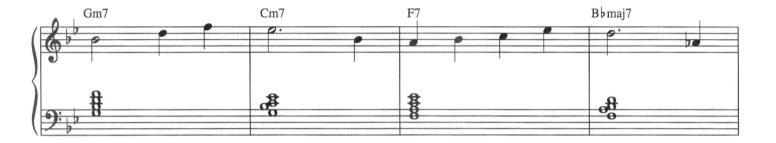

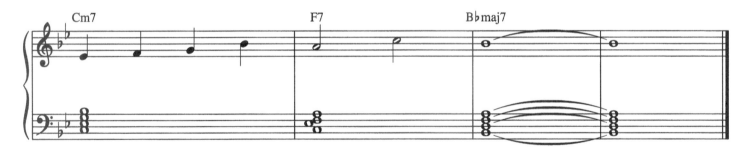

Create a swing version of "All The Moon And Things."

CHORD MELODY

Melody and chords can be played at the same time by the right hand while the left hand plays a bass part. The following example illustrates a simple way of doing this for "All the Moon and Things."

4. RH CHORD MELODY
LH ROOTS

Use the following procedure to play a simple chord melody version:

RULES: Play a close position chord with the melody note as the top voice on the first beat of each new chord change. Play each chord only once and play any additional melody notes in the measure as single notes.

Play the root of each new chord change with the left hand.

When the first melody note with a new chord is not a chord tone, but the following note is a chord tone, leave that chord tone (resolution note) out of the voicing, as the melody will resolve to it (see measures 17, 19, 21, 23).

When the first melody note with a new chord has been tied, play the remaining chord tones below while tying the melody note (see measures 18, 20, 22, 24).

Fig. 10-5 All the Moon and Things

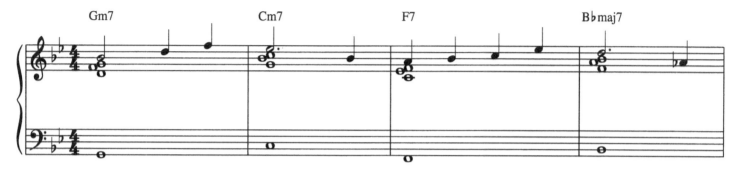

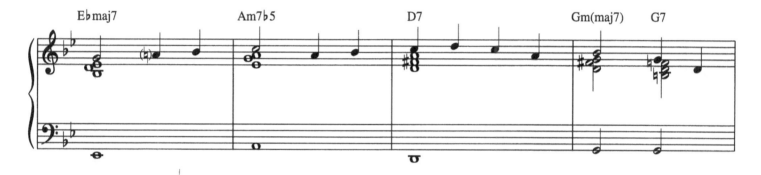

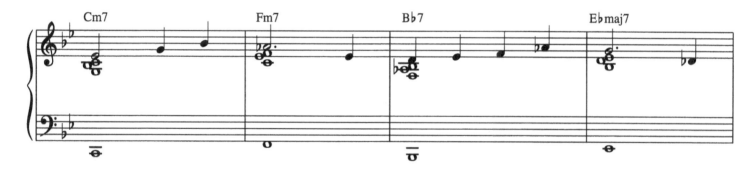

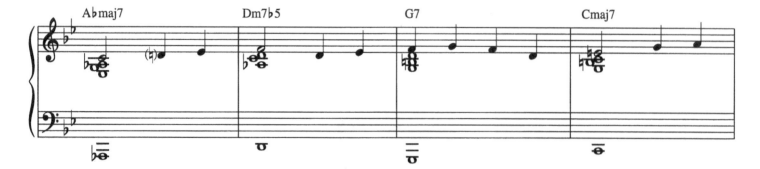

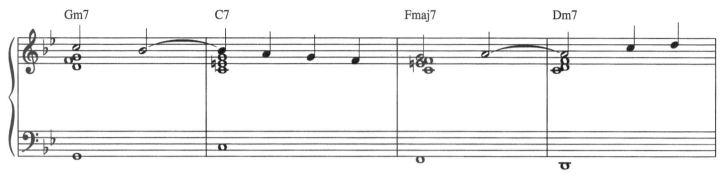

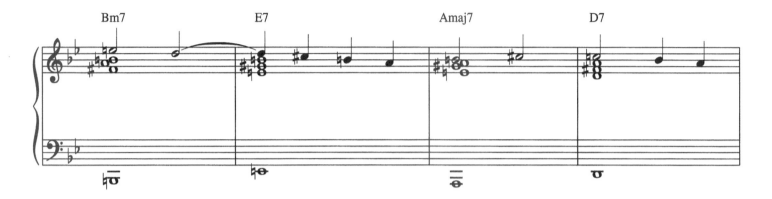

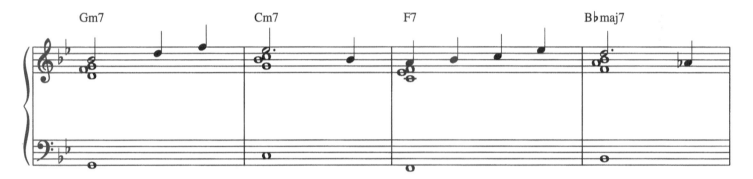

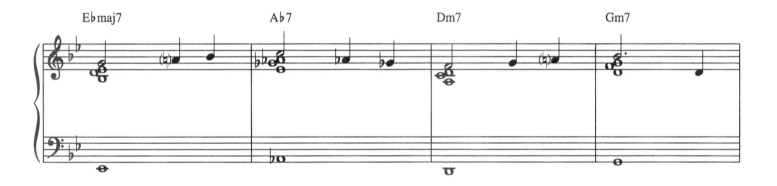

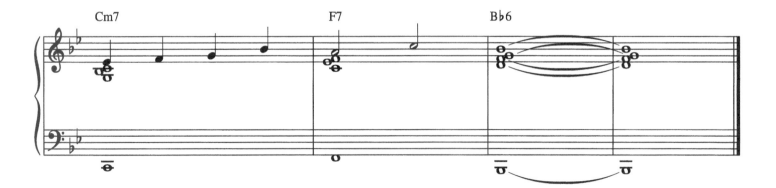

LESSON 11
COMBINED CLOSE POSITION FORMULAS
JAZZ WALTZ

A jazz waltz is a tune in three-four time played with a swing feel. Various waltz patterns can be used in the left hand. Swing eighth notes are used in both hands.

HOMILY

"Homily" is a jazz waltz that contains chord progressions based on II-V-I, II-V, and Circle of Fifths progressions. See p. 145 of the Appendix for the lead sheet. In triple meter, when there are two chords in a measure, the second chord is usually played on the third beat unless otherwise indicated. Play "Homily" in the following ways:

1. RH CHORDS
LH ROOTS

Use both **CPF1** and **CPF2**. In the example below, the formulas were chosen for their position in the center of the keyboard and for smooth voice leading. Other alternatives are possible and should be tried.

Fig. 11-1 Homily

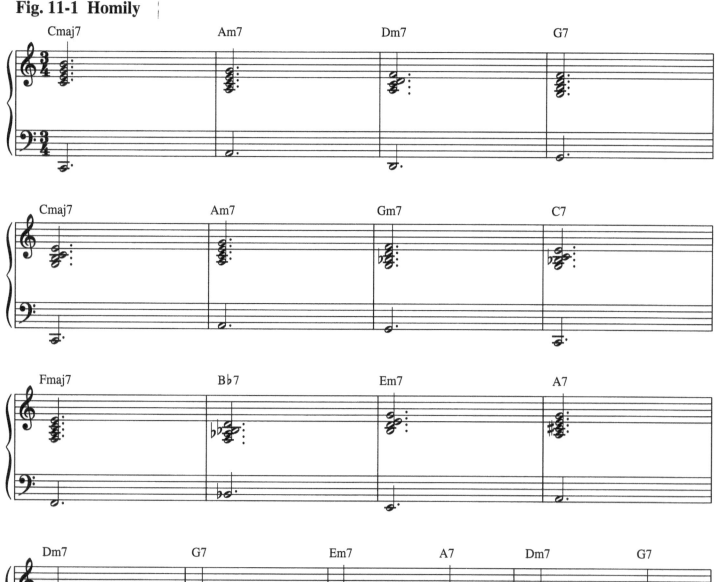

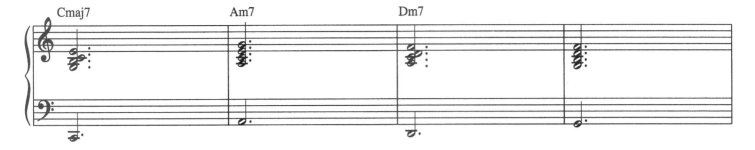

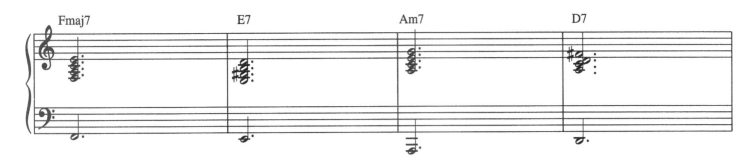

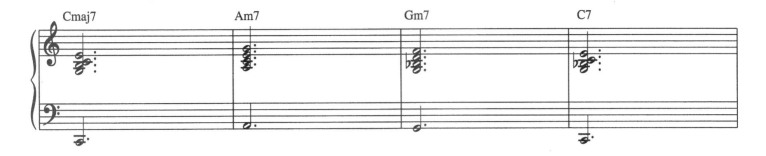

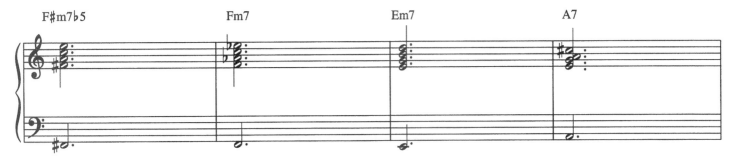

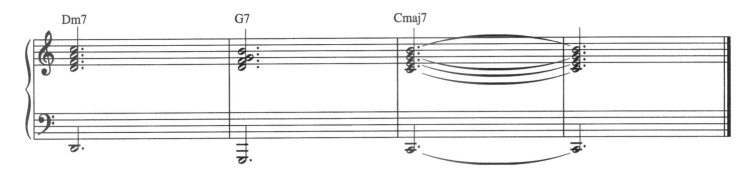

JAZZ WALTZ PATTERNS
2. RH CHORDS
LH ROOTS

Play the chords as before but in the "simple" jazz waltz rhythm shown below. The chords in the right hand are played with a swing feel and a gentle lilting feeling should be produced.

Fig. 11-2 Homily

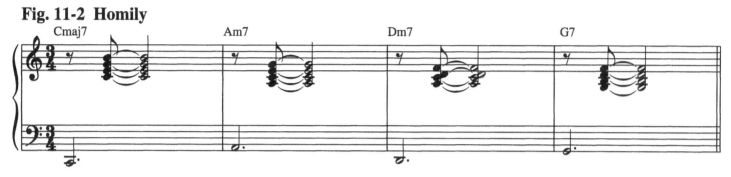

3. RH MELODY
LH CHORDS (JAZZ WALTZ PATTERNS)

Play the melody in the right hand and the simple jazz waltz pattern in the left hand. Separate the root from the rest of the chord as demonstrated below. All chords with a duration of three or two beats are in root position. Chords with a duration of one beat are inverted (see measures 15-16). Practice the left hand alone before adding the melody.

Fig. 11-3 Homily

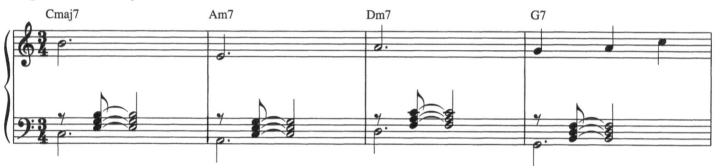

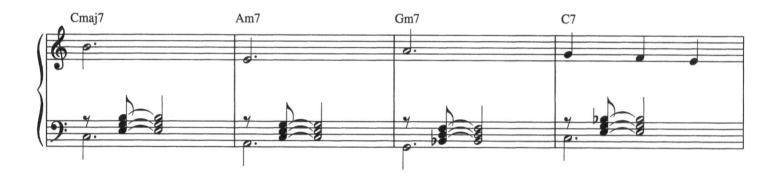

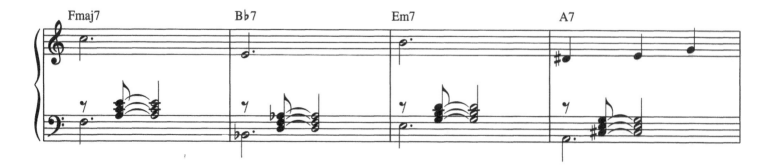

Continue...

Apply the following patterns to the left hand. For each example, practice the left hand alone before adding the melody in the right hand. The first one below is the same as the one above.

Fig. 11-4A

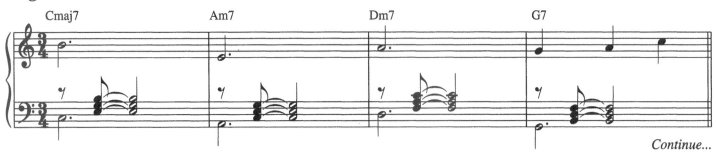

Continue...

Fig. 11-4B

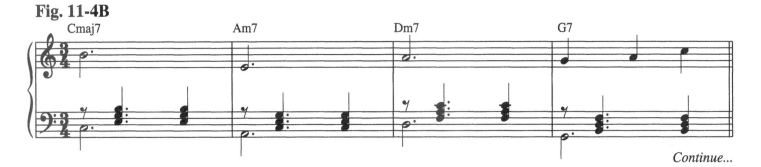

Continue...

Fig. 11-4C

Continue...

Fig. 11-4D

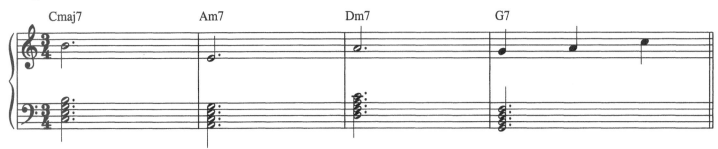

Continue...

Fig. 11-4E

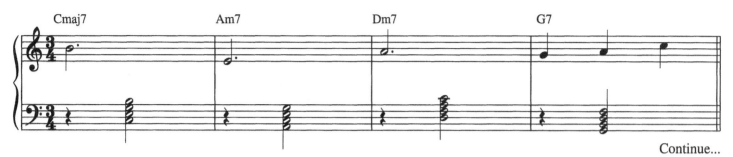

Continue...

Fig. 11-4F

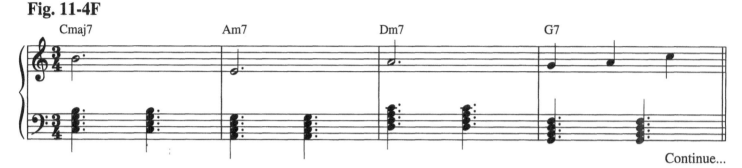

Continue...

Fig. 11-4G

Continue...

4. RH MELODY
LH CHORDS - NO FIFTHS

Close position chords often sound too dense and cluttered. In most situations, the fifth of any chord can be eliminated without affecting the quality of the chord since it is mainly the third and the seventh that determine the quality. Minor seventh flat five and diminished chords are sometimes an exception since the flat fifth determines the quality of the chord along with the third and seventh.

Play Jazz Waltz Pattern 1 as before but eliminate the fifth from each chord as shown below. This creates a more open sound that lightens the music considerably. Open voicings will be discussed in Chapter 13.

Fig. 11-5

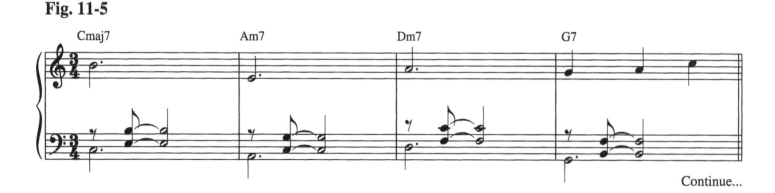

Continue...

Try the same procedure with Patterns 2 and 3.

5. RH MELODY
LH COMBINED JAZZ WALTZ PATTERNS

Play "Homily" by mixing all of the patterns throughout the tune. Eliminate the fifths of each chord. There are many possible ways of mixing the patterns and the reader should invent and improvise others after playing the example.

Fig. 11-6 Homily

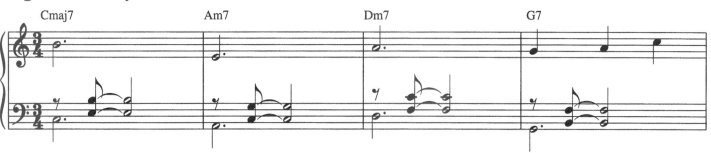

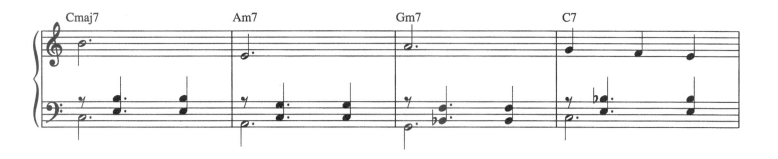

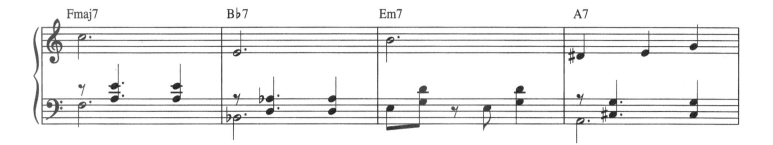

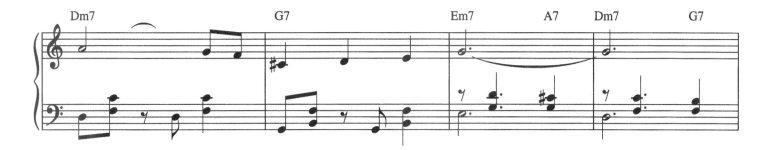

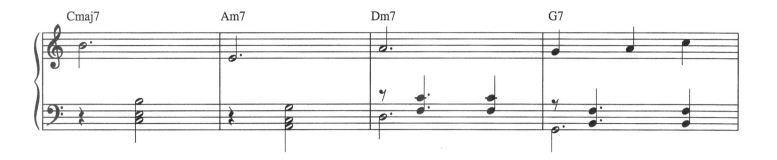

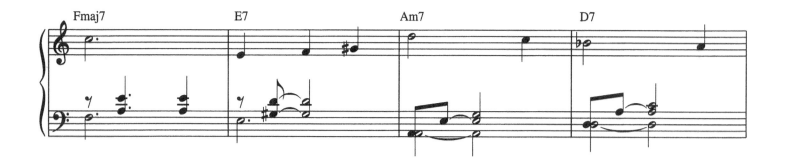

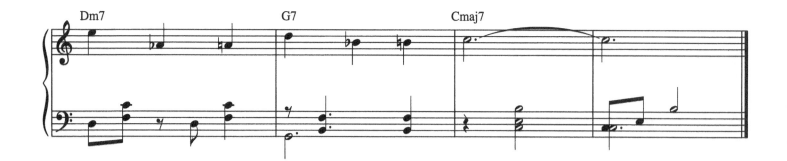

LESSON 12
DIMINISHED SEVENTH CHORDS
DOMINANT FLAT NINE CHORDS
SUSPENSIONS
DIMINISHED SEVENTH CHORDS

Diminished seventh chords are not strictly part of the diatonic system for major keys. Because of this, they are useful in creating a sense of ambiguity. A single diminished seventh chord can have several implied resolutions and, therefore, can take a chord progression to unexpected places. A diminished seventh chord is a symmetrical chord since all of the notes within the chord are a minor third apart. Inversions of diminished seventh chords are really just the same as other root position diminished seventh chords. A Cdim7 chord (C-E♭-G♭-A) inverts to an E♭dim7, a G♭dim7, and an Adim7.

Fig. 12-1

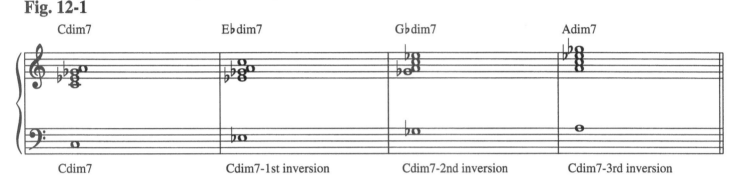

Cdim7   Cdim7-1st inversion   Cdim7-2nd inversion   Cdim7-3rd inversion

DOMINANT FLAT NINE CHORDS

Extensions are often added to basic seventh chords. These extensions are acquired by using notes that add thirds above the seventh. The choice of thirds used can vary for each type of chord. A common extended chord is the dominant flat nine chord. It is structured by adding a note that is a minor third above the seventh of a dominant seventh chord. The natural ninth is equivalent to a major second above the root (but an octave higher). The flatted ninth is equivalent to a minor second above the root. A G7♭9 chord is spelled G-B-D-F-A♭.

Since we are only playing full chords in one hand for now, a flat nine chord can only be played by substituting the flatted ninth for the root. This works fine when chords are played in the right hand and the roots are played in the left hand.

Fig. 12-2

Flat nine chords can easily be inserted in the close position formulas **CPF1** and **CPF2**. Play the flatted ninth instead of the root in the right hand.

Fig. 12-3

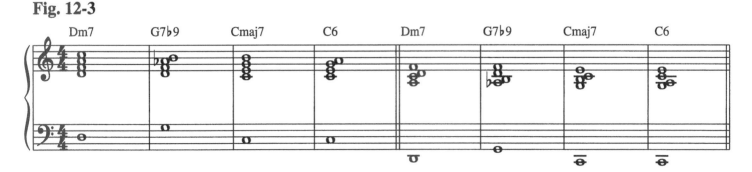

Fig. 12-4

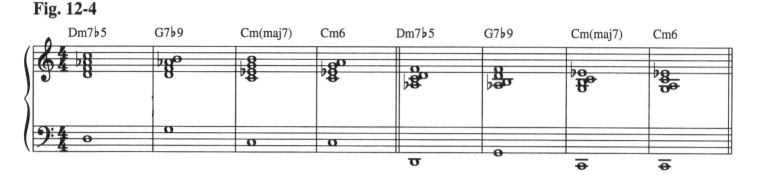

BOSSA-NOVA

Bossa-nova is a style of jazz that blends elements of jazz and Brazilian rhythms. Latin American music is an important part of jazz and aspects of bossa-nova presented in this lesson can be applied to other forms of Latin influenced jazz. Bossa-nova is characterized by a complex, syncopated, underlying rhythm pattern that accompanies a simple or complex melodic rhythm. All Latin music is based on straight eighth note rhythms. An underlying pulse of eight notes per measure is felt along with the basic quarter note pulse. This is true of rock related music as well.

BOSSATION

The essential quality of Latin music is the layering of rhythm patterns. These patterns may be consistent or random. The example below presents a consistent rhythm pattern that can be used as an accompaniment for "Bossation." See p. 152 of the Appendix for the lead sheet.

1. RH CHORDS (BOSSA-NOVA PATTERN)
LH BASS

Most bass parts for Latin jazz are based on the root and fifth of each chord in a chord progression. In the next example, the left hand plays the root and fifth of each chord as constant half notes. The right hand plays a more complex pattern that repeats every two measures. The following two measures may serve as an introduction to the tune.

Fig. 12-5

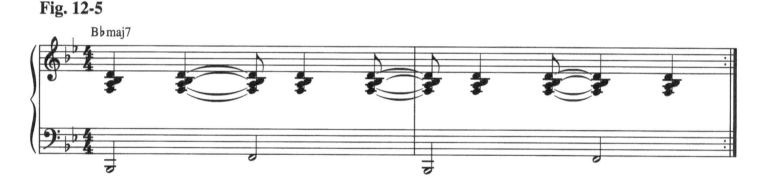

Play through "Bossation" as an accompaniment. Follow the rules below:

RULES: Play the root then fifth of each chord as half notes in the left hand when the chord lasts for one or more measures. Keep the notes fairly low in register.

Play the chords in the right hand keeping the same two measure rhythm pattern as above. If there is a chord change within the rhythm pattern, anticipate the new chord by playing it an eighth note before the downbeat when the root of that chord is played by the left hand (see measures 7-8 and 11-12).

The voicings chosen in the example below make use of **CPF2.** If "Bossation" were played in another key, **CPF1** or a combination might be more suitable. In this key the chords lay well in the middle area of the keyboard and **CPF2** works well. Observe and play all diminished and flat nine chords.

Fig. 12-6 Bossation

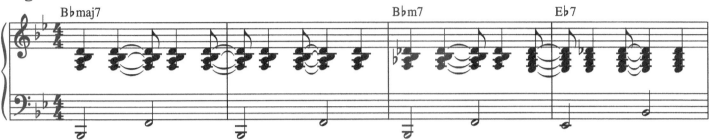

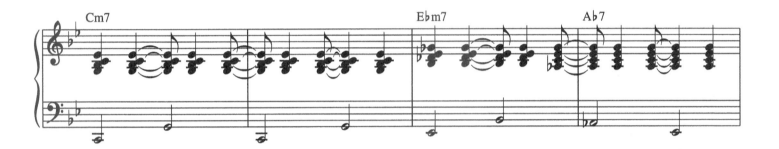

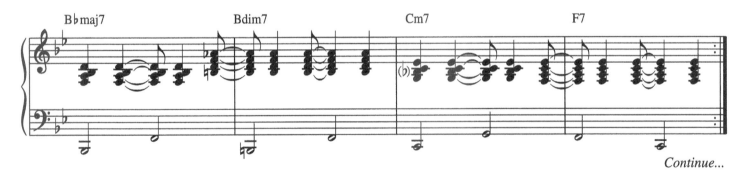

Continue...

2. RH MELODY
LH BASS

Play the melody in the right hand and use the same bass part as before.

Fig. 12-7 Bossation

Continue...

3. RH MELODY AND CHORDS (BOSSA-NOVA RHYTHM)
LH BASS

This procedure combines aspects of chord melody playing (see Lesson 9) and the procedures presented on pages 64 and 65. Follow the rules below.

Before playing the chords in the right hand in a bossa-nova rhythm, play a simple chord melody. Play a close-position chord with the melody note as the top voice on the first beat of each new chord change. In this particular tune, first and third inversion chords are necessary to accommodate the melody. Notice the use of a sharp nine chord in measure 16.

Fig. 12-8 Bossation

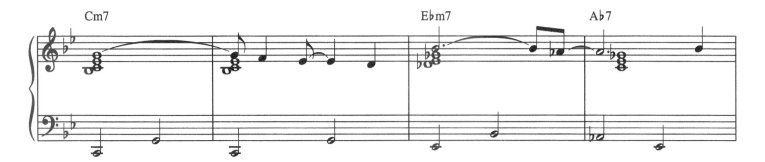

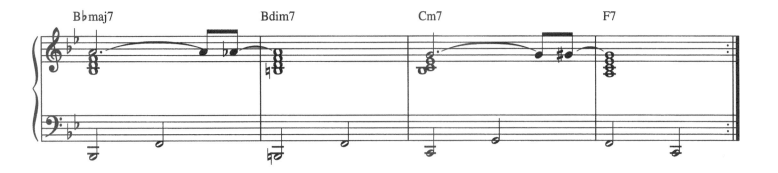

Follow the rules below to play melody, bass, and chords in rhythm at the same time. Since all three parts cannot always be played at the same time, certain compromises must be made. The overall feeling of all parts can be maintained even though the chord rhythm may be missing at times.

RULES: Play a close position chord below the first melody note of each new chord change. If the melody note lasts for several beats, sustain the melody note and "plug into" the bossa-nova rhythm with the underlying three notes. When the melody becomes more active, sustain the chord while playing the melody notes.

Fig. 12-9 Bossation

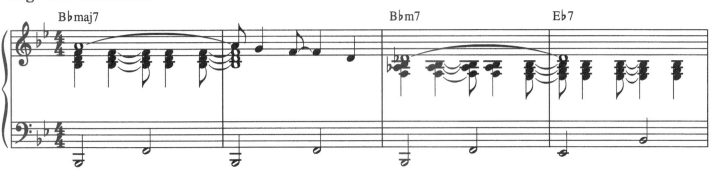

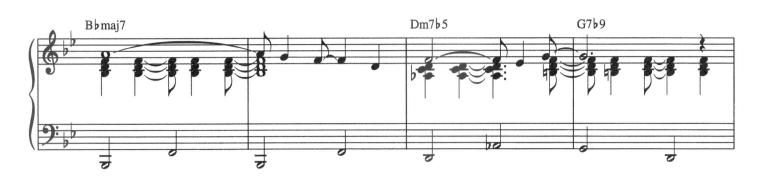

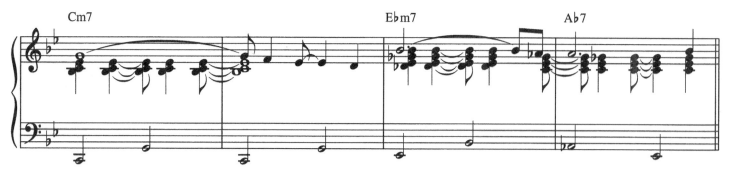

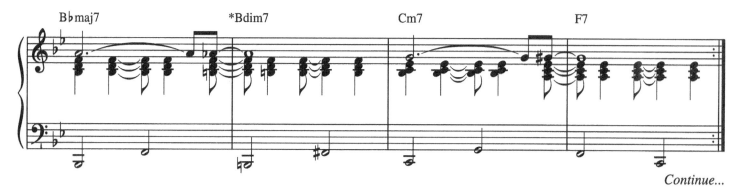

Continue...

*Diminished seventh chords are often used to connect chords that are a whole step apart.

SUSPENSIONS

Traditional theory defines a suspension as a prepared dissonant note or non-chord tone that resloves stepwise to a chord tone. Jazz treats suspensions as notes that require neither preparation nor resolution. The fourth of a dominant seventh chord is usually the suspended tone and is used in place of the third in what is called a dominant seventh sus four chord.

Fig. 12-10

Suspensions can be prepared in II-V progressions by holding the II chord (minor seventh) over when the root changes for the V chord (dominant seventh). This process yields a Dm7 over a G bass note which can be written as Dm7/G. The resulting suspended chord is technically a G9sus4. The ninth results from carrying over the fifth of the II chord (A natural). The chord spelling Dm7/G is a useful way of indicating a suspended dominant chord. The root of the chord is G and the chord really is a G9sus4 and not a Dm7.

Fig. 12-11

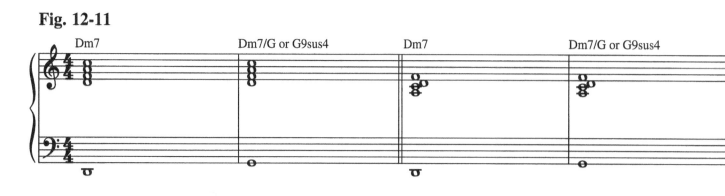

The suspension used above can be resolved by changing to the V chord while the root of the V chord still sounds.

Fig. 12-12

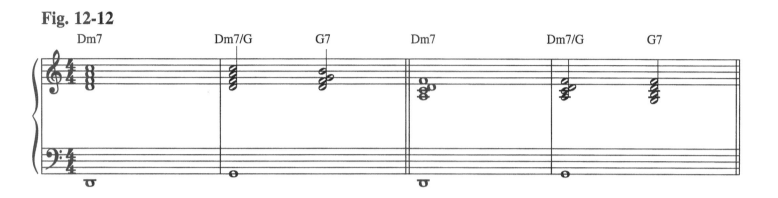

Suspensions can be played without preparation.

Fig. 12-13

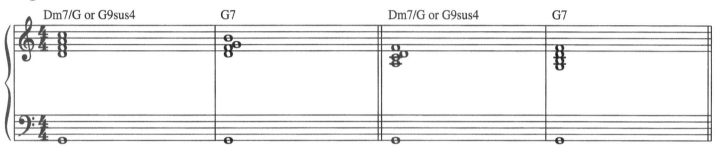

Suspensions can be played without resolution to the third of the dominant chord.

Fig. 12-14

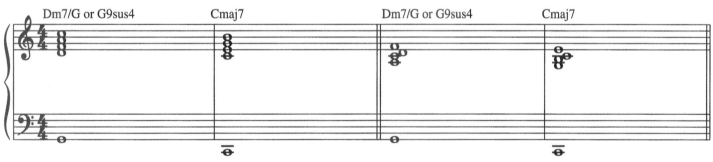

The examples below demonstrate how these procedures can be played by the left hand alone.

Fig. 12-15

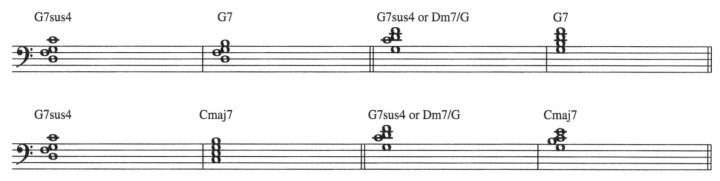

Suspensions are often indicated in music and should be played accordingly.

Fig. 12-16

II-V progressions can be turned into suspensions, when appropriate, by using the procedures above. The example below shows how this can be done in "Lunar Eclipse."

Fig. 12-17

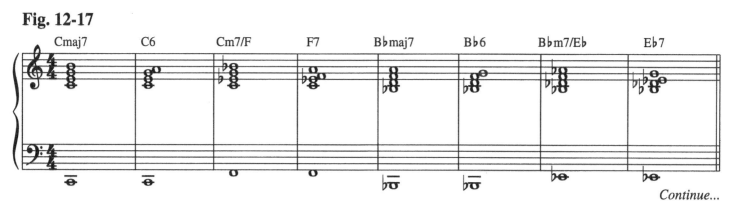

Continue...

Play the melody of "Lunar Eclipse" in the right hand and use the suspended chords in the left hand.

Suspensions can be created in "Bossation" by playing the root and fifth of the V chord under the II chord that proceeds the V chord in any of the II-V progressions. Play the accompaniment again using suspensions as below.

Fig. 12-18

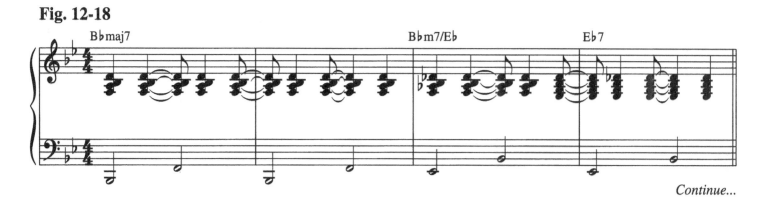

Continue...

SECTION 2
LESSON 13
OPEN POSITION 1 VOICINGS

Open voicings are chord voicings that contain gaps between adjacent chord tones. All chord tones are used, but they are not always arranged in sequential order. Close Position 1 (see Lesson 1) voices all available chord tones in sequential order from the bottom up: 1-3-5-7. For Open Position 1, the chords are voiced from the bottom up as 1-7-3-5.

The third and the fifth are removed from the middle and placed on top. Two hands are required to play open voicings. For Open Position 1, the left hand plays 1-7 and the right hand plays 3-5.

Fig. 13-1

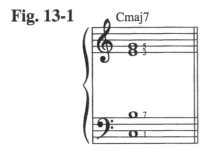

DIATONIC SEVENTH CHORDS
MAJOR KEYS

Practice diatonic seventh chords in all major keys using Open Position Formula 1. Play through one octave, ascending and descending. The keys of C and G major are presented below. Play in all keys. Play in the same order as the close position diatonic seventh chords: **C, G, F, D, B♭, A, E♭, E, A♭, B, D♭, G♭.** If necessary, refer to the Diatonic Seventh Chords written in close position in the Appendix.

Fig. 13-2

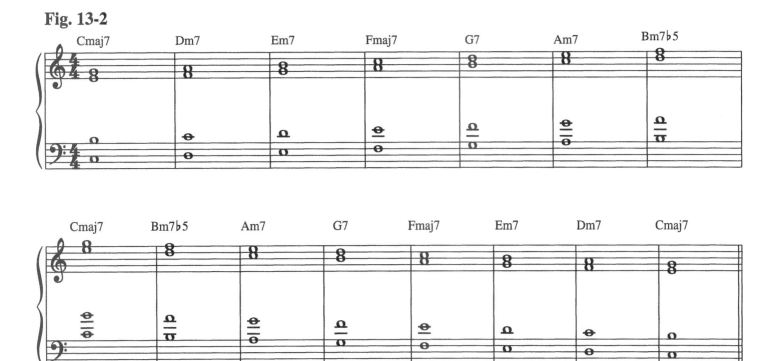

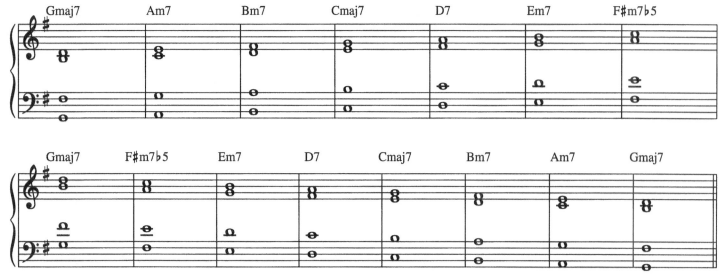

Continue in all major keys...

OPEN POSITION FORMULA 1
MAJOR KEYS

A smooth voice leading formula for Open Position 1 can be applied to II-V-I progressions. The formula below represents a simple, smooth, and efficient way to play a II-V-I in C major.

Fig. 13-3

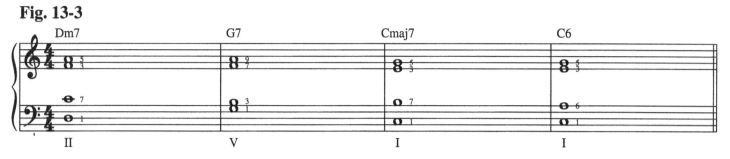

The II and the I chords use Open Position Voicing 1: 1-7-3-5. The V chord, however, uses a 1-3-7-9 voicing. Since only four notes are used, the fifth is eliminated from the voicing. The movement to and from the V chord is very smooth and convenient. It also sounds good. Ninths are common in jazz and they will be used throughout the rest of the book. Notice that the major ninth is used here.

The right hand has little to think about once the third and fifth is located for the II chord. It plays the same notes for the V chord, which become 7-9, then they move down stepwise in the key for the 3-5 of the I chords. The left hand moves in a similar way as it did for **CPF1,** only now leaving notes out. This voicing formula is easy to master if one already has mastered **CPF1.**

Fingering for the left hand is very important in this system. The II and I chords should always use fingers 5 and 1, and the V chord should always use fingers 2 and 1. This fingering is similar to the fingering used for **CPF1.** This fingering also places the fingers in good position to play the next voicing.

Practice II-V-I progression in all major keys using Open Position Formula 1 - **OPF1.**

Fig. 13-4

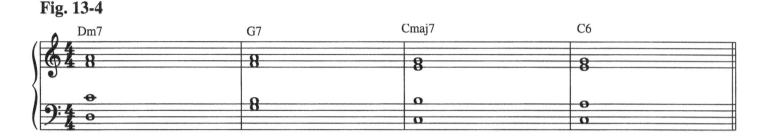

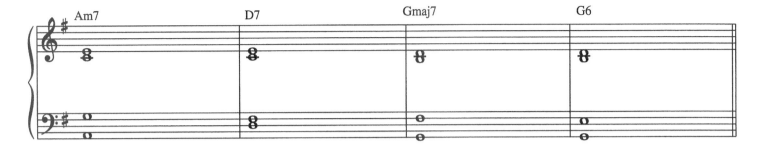

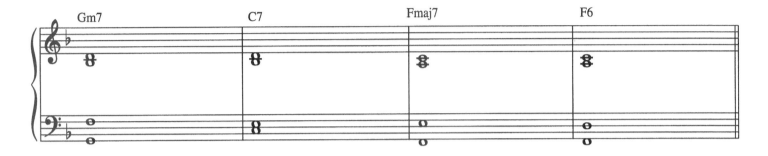

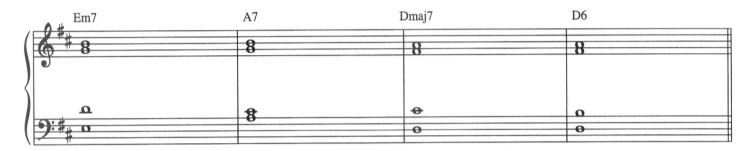

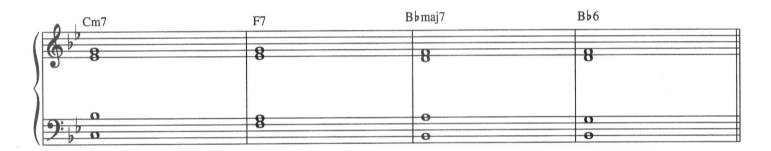

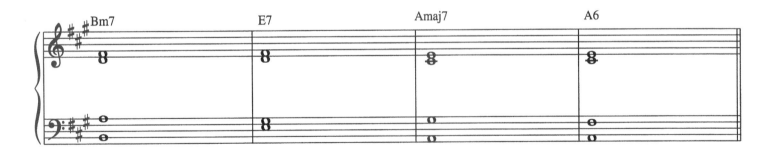

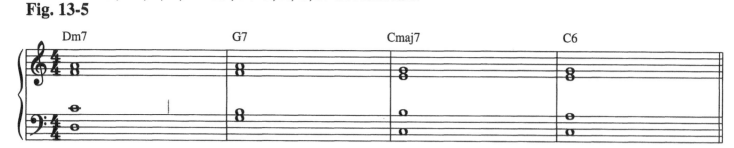

OPF1 can be practiced in two cycles of descending whole steps, as was done with the close-position formulas. The following order of keys in each cycle should be used: C, B♭, A♭, G♭, E, D, and E♭, D♭ B, A, G, F. See Lesson 2.

Fig. 13-5

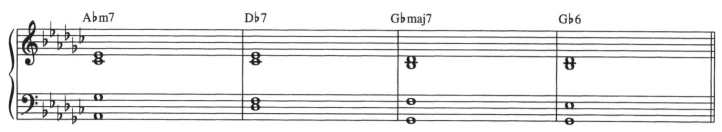

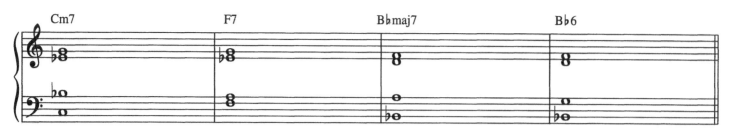

Continue...

II-V progressions which resolve to another II-V progression should be practiced in two cycles of descending whole steps. See Lesson 2.

Fig. 13-6

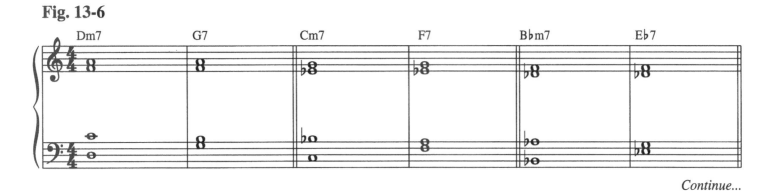

Continue...

Often a flat ninth is used on a V chord in a major II-V-I or II-V progression. The fifth of the II chord now moves down by half-step to the flat ninth of the V chord. Practice in all ways presented above. Continue the following examples

Fig. 13-7

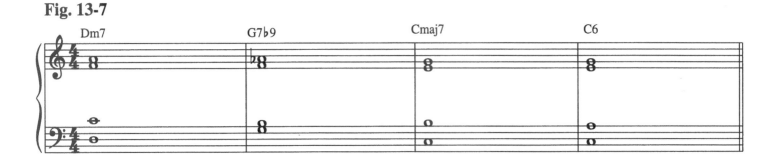

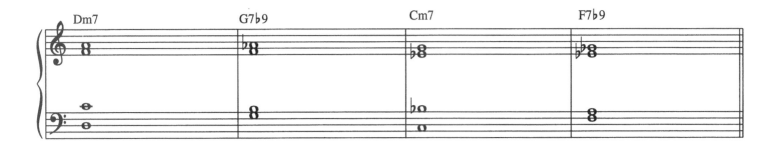

OPEN POSITION FORMULA 1
MINOR KEYS

Open Position Formula 1 can also be applied to minor II-V-I and II-V progressions. The same principles and voicing leading motions are used in both major and minor tonalities.

Fig. 13-8

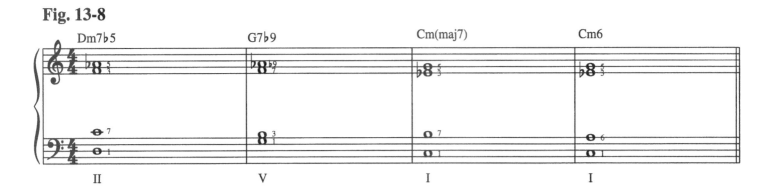

Notice that the flat fifth of the II chord turns into the flat ninth of the V chord. Practice **OPF1** in all minor keys in the same ways as previously done with major keys. See Lesson 4 for whole step cycles for minor keys.

Fig. 13-9

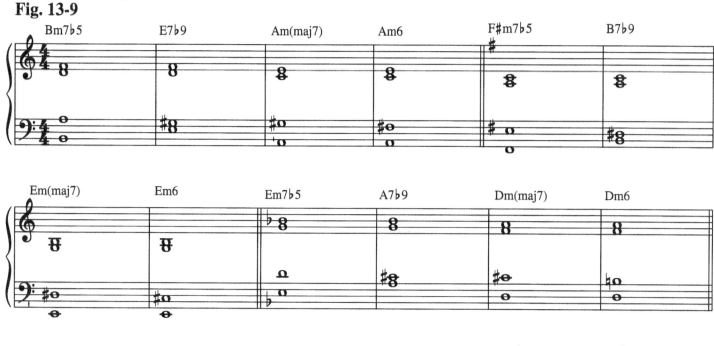

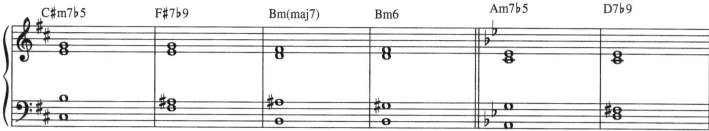

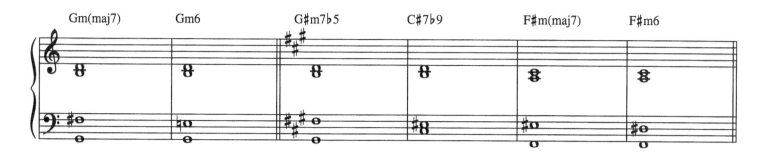

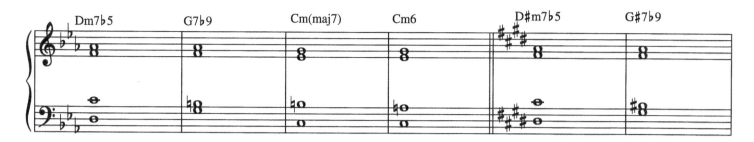

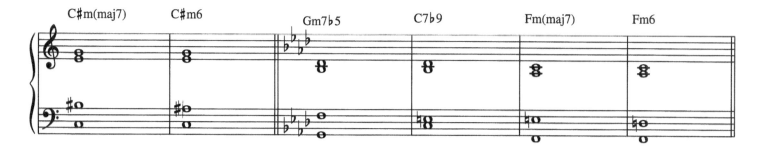

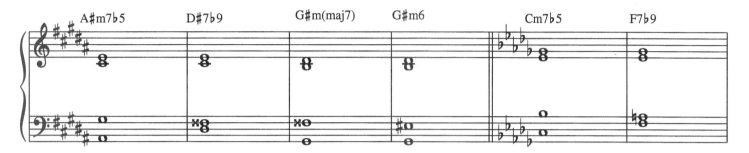

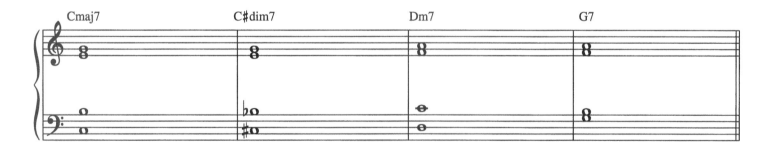

OPEN POSITION 1 VOICINGS
DIMINISHED SEVENTH CHORDS

Open position 1 voicings can be easily used for diminished seventh chords. Two examples are presented below.

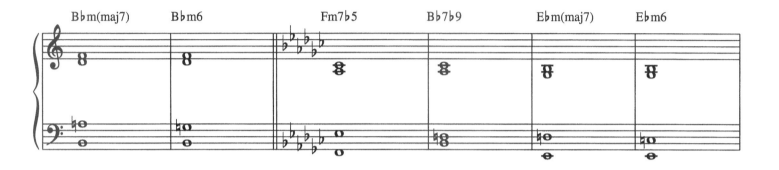

LESSON 14
APPLYING OPEN POSITION FORMULA 1

Open position chords can be used for playing tunes as well as chord changes. Applying open position voicings presents more of a problem than applying closed position voicings since both hands are required to play open position voicings. The hands are no longer separated into specific roles such as RH melody with LH chords, or RH chords with LH bass. This lesson will offer specific guidelines for the rendering of tunes using Open Position 1 voicings and Open Position Formula 1. The tunes used are ones that have already been presented and the reader should be familiar with them and their harmonic structures and motions. See p. 146 of the Appendix for the lead sheet.

LUNAR ECLIPSE

"Lunar Eclipse" should be played in the following three ways:

1. OPEN VOICES WITH BOTH HANDS

Play through the chord changes using Open Position 1 voicings and Open Position Formula 1 when it applies. Use **OPF1** for all II-V-I and II-V progressions in the same manner that **CPF1** was used in Chapter 3. Although the voicings are different from before, the two new alternative open voicing possibilities, 1-7-3-5 and 1-3-7-9, can be related directly to the close-position-root-position and second-inversion voicings, respectively. All chords that were previously voiced in root position are now voiced 1-7-3-5, and all chords previously voiced in second inversion are now voiced 1-3-7-9.

Fig. 14-1

Continue...

2. RH MELODY
LH VOICINGS (2 notes)

Play the melody in single notes with the right hand while using the two-note voicing in the left hand.

Fig. 14-2

Continue...

3. RH MELODY
LH-RH VOICINGS

This step combines the two previous steps. Play the melody with the right hand while playing the full voicings with both hands (two notes with each hand). This procedure ideally leads to a five note texture; one melody note accompanied by four chord tones. Although this is almost always possible in "Lunar Eclipse," it may not always be so for other tunes. These exceptions will be discussed in the next lesson.

The right hand performs two distinct functions, melody and voicing, and it is important to keep these separate. A chord voicing may be necessary on the first beat of a measure, even though there may be a rest in the melody part. While playing this full version of melody and chords at the same time, fingering for the melody may be quite different for the right hand than it is when playing just single notes. Because two notes are often held while the melody proceeds, it is often necessary to play several successive melody notes with the fifth finger. This may be awkward at first, but playing through several tunes this way should make it more natural.

Fig. 14-3

Continue...

4. SWING FEEL
RH MELODY
LH-RH VOICINGS

Play as above but with a swing feel (see Lesson #7). Continue the example below in a similar style. Be careful to separate the voicing from the melody in the right hand.

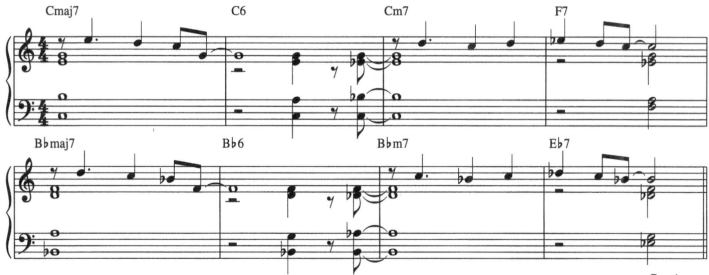

Continue...

LESSON 15
OPEN POSITION FORMULA 1
CIRCLE OF FIFTH PROGRESSIONS

The principle at work in **OPF1** can be applied to any root movement around the circle of descending fifths. A similar application of this principle was used with closed position voicings in Lesson 6. Review Lesson 6 for an explanation of circle of fifths progressions before proceeding with this lesson.

The examples below present **OPF1** voicings for the same chord patterns presented in Lesson 6. They illustrate circle of fifths progressions that isolate a particular chord quality. 1-7-3-5 voicings will alternate with 1-3-7-9 voicings. Two cycles are presented for each exercise in order to accommodate all possible combinations.

II-IV PROGRESSIONS —
MAJOR SEVENTH CHORD MOVEMENT

Fig. 15-1

III-VI PROGRESSIONS –
MINOR SEVENTH CHORD MOVEMENT

Fig. 15-2

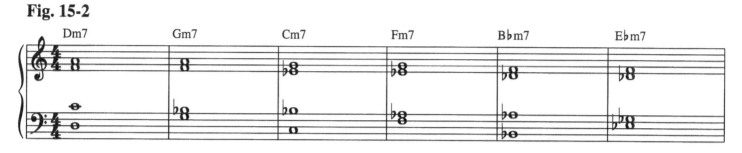

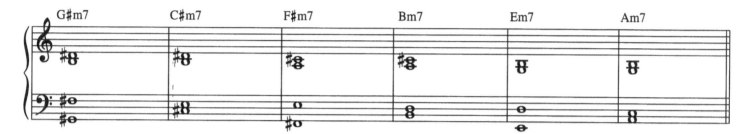

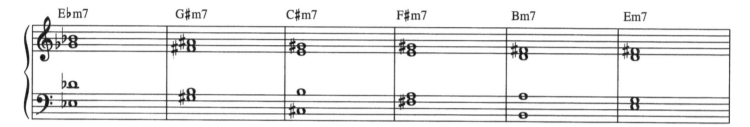

V OF V PROGRESSIONS–
DOMINANT SEVENTH CHORD MOVEMENT

Fig. 15-3

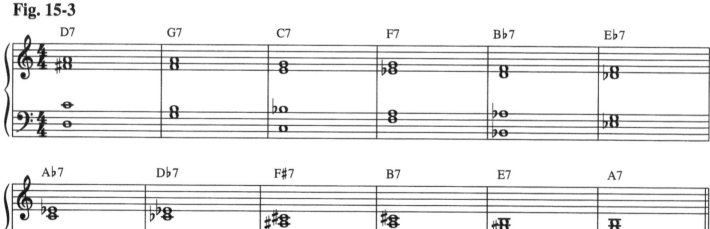

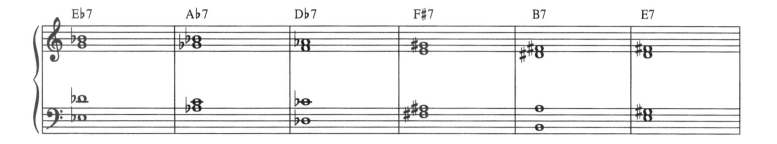

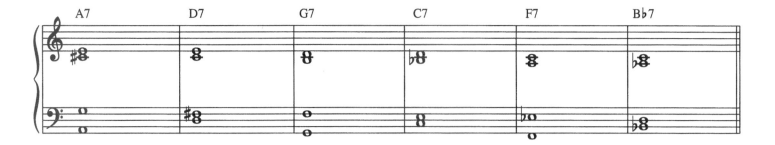

AUTUMN WONDERLAND

"Autumn Wonderland" makes use of all the previous progressions, as well as II-V-I and II-V progressions in major and minor. See Lesson 6 for an analysis of this tune. As before, there is a direct correspondence between the closed position voicing used in Lesson 6 and the open position voicings used here. All chords that were previously voiced in root position are now voiced 1-7-3-5, and all chords previously voiced in second inversion are now voiced 1-3-7-9.

Play "Autumn Wonderland" in the same three ways as "Lunar Eclipse" in Lesson 14. Use **OPF1** when applicable.

1. OPEN VOICES WITH BOTH HANDS

Fig. 15-4

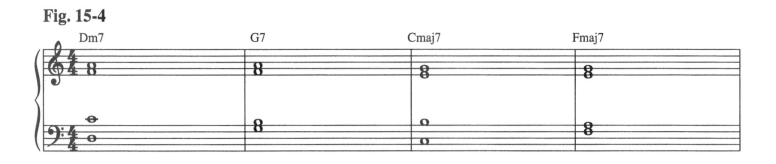

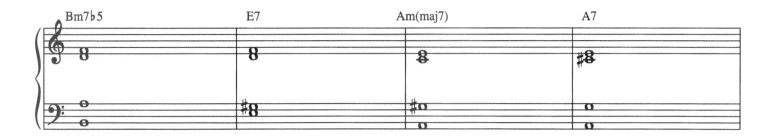

Continue...

2. RH MELODY
LH VOICINGS (2 notes)

Fig. 15-5

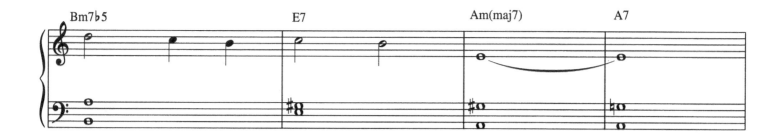

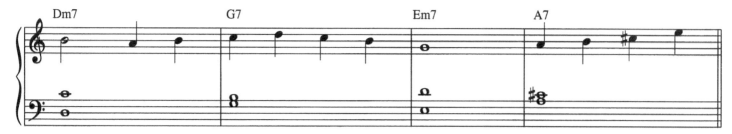

Continue...

3. RH MELODY
LH-RH VOICINGS

Although the ideal texture for this voicing system is that of a melody and a four note voicing (five notes altogether), it is not always possible in certain situations. The melody note should always be the uppermost voice in this system and sometimes notes must be left out of the voicing to accommodate the melody. This often happens when the melody note is the fifth (or lower) of a II or I chord, or the ninth or root of a V chord. Use the following rules for "Autumn Wonderland:"

RULES: When a melody note interferes with a note or notes of a voicing, leave the note(s) out of the voicing (see measures 9-11 and 15).

When a melody note proceeds to the top note of a voicing immediately after the chord is played, it is best to delete that note from the initial voicing (see measure 12-13).

Fig. 15-6

Continue...

Try to play "Autumn Wonderland" with a swing feel. Refer to "Lunar Eclipse" in Lesson 14.

LESSON 16
OPEN POSITION 2 VOICINGS

There are many possible ways of voicing a chord. This lesson presents another common open-position voicing. Open Position 2 voicings are characterized by the use of open fifths in the left hand and open fifths or fourths in the right hand. The left hand always plays the root and fifth, 1- 5, and the right hand plays the third and seventh, either as 3-7 or 7-3. Thus, there are two possible Open Position 2 voicings.

Fig. 16-1

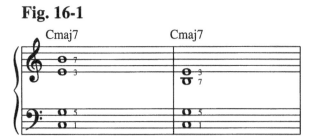

Open Position 2 voicings should be practiced as diatonic seventh chords in all keys. Play in the same order as the close position diatonic seventh chords: **C, G, F, D, B♭, A, E♭, E, A♭, B, D♭, G♭.** If necessary, refer to the Diatonic Seventh Chords written in close position in the Appendix.

Below are the two possible voicings of diatonic seventh chords for the keys of C and F major.

Fig. 16-2
C Major 1-5-3-7

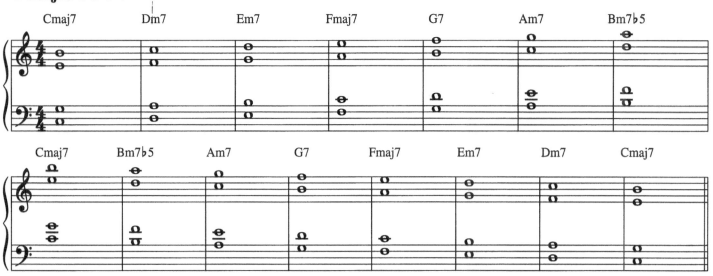

C Major 1-5-7-3

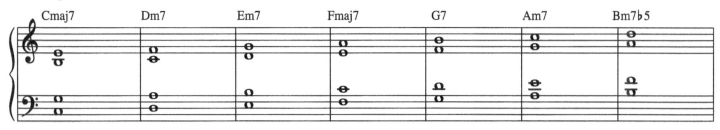

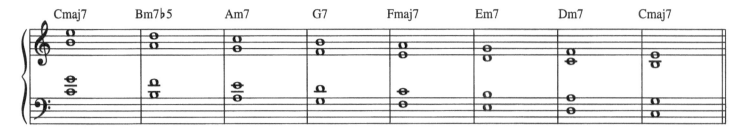

Fig. 16-3

F Major 1-5-3-7

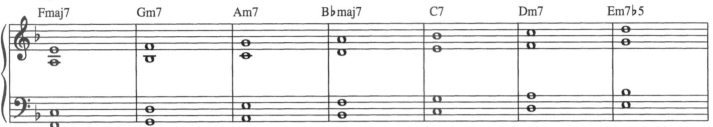

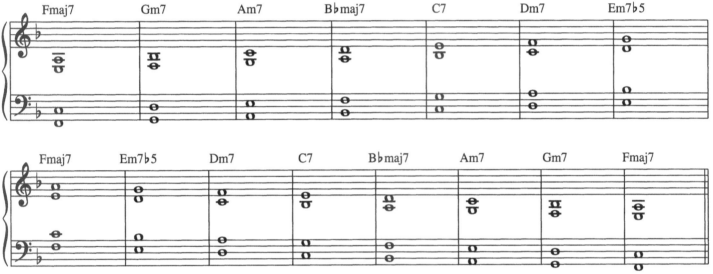

F Major 1-5-7-3

Continue in all major keys.

OPEN POSITION FORMULA 2
MAJOR KEYS

A relatively smooth voice leading formula for Open Position 2 can be appled to a II-V-I progression, as was done in **OPF1**. The examples below present the two possibilities for Open Position Formula 2 (**OPF2**). The left hand is always the same since it always plays 1-5. The right hand plays 3-7 on the II chord, which moves to 7-3 on the V chord, which then moves to 3-7 and 3-6 on the I chord. For the alternative possibility, the right hand plays 7-3 on the II chord, which moves to 3-7 on the V chord, which then moves to 7-3 and 6-3 on the I chord. All voicing principles that apply to the seventh apply to the sixth as well.

Fig. 16-4

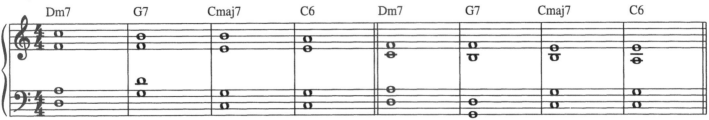

88

The following lists II-V-I progressions in all major keys using both versions of **OPF2**. Practice as before.

Fig. 16-5

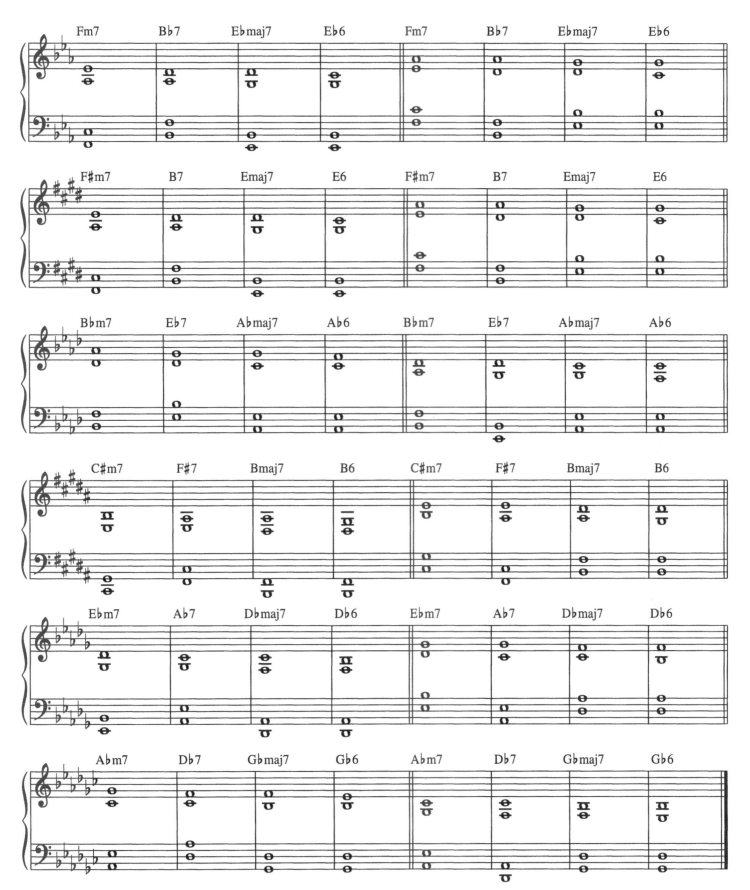

OPF2 can be practiced in two cycles of descending whole steps. Alternating II-V progresssions should be practiced as before. The following order in each cycle should be used: C, Bb, Ab, Gb, E, D and Eb, Db, B, A, G, F.

Play through II-V-I and alternating II-V progressions with each version of **OPF2** using the whole step cycles as before. See Lesson 2.

OPEN POSITION FORMULA 2
MINOR KEYS

Open Position Formula 2 can be applied to minor II-V-I and II-V progressions as well as to major keys. The same principles and voicing leading motions are used in both situations.

Fig. 16-6

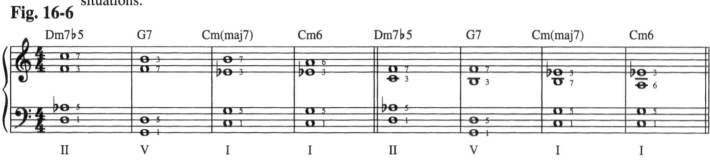

Practice **OPF2** in all minor keys in all of the same ways as the major keys above. **OPF2** in all minor keys is listed below. See Lesson 4 for descending whole step cycles for minor keys.

Fig. 16-7

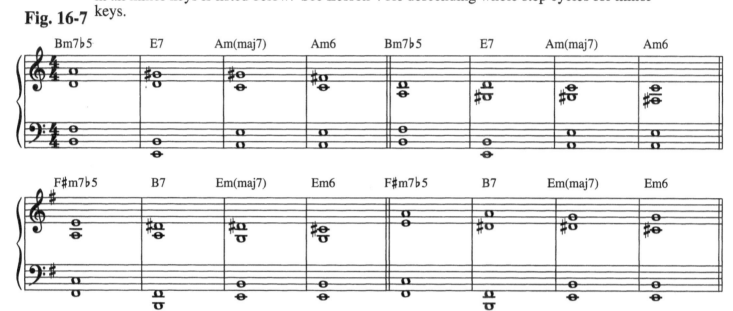

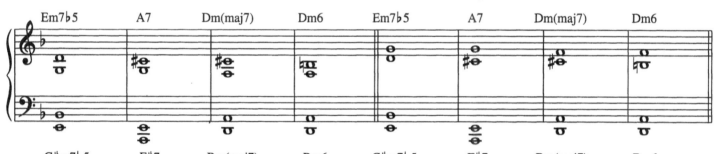

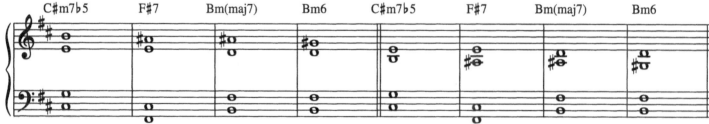

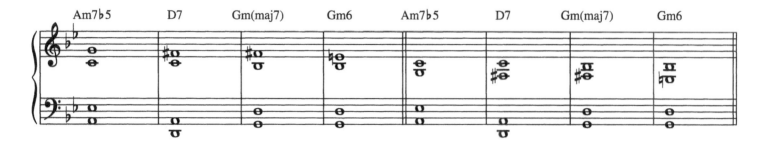

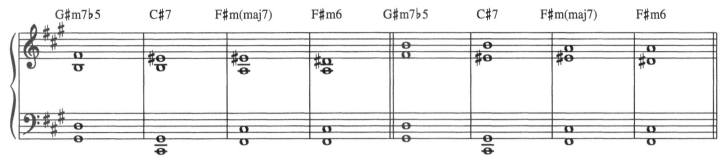

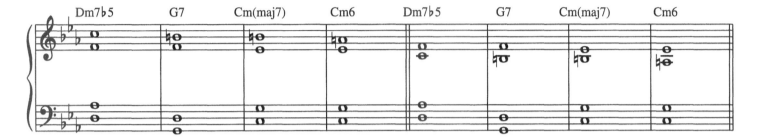

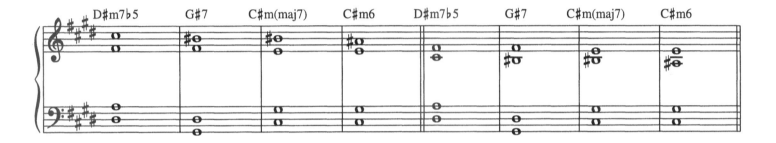

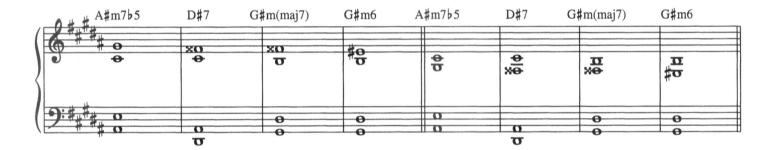

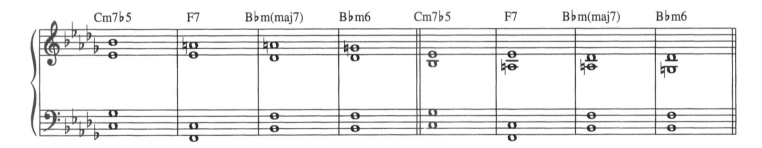

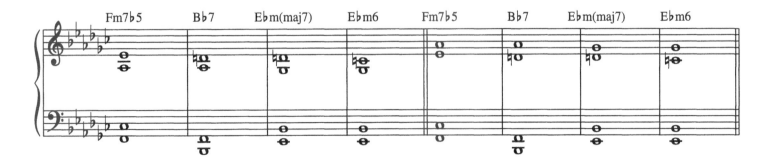

LESSON 17
APPLYING OPEN POSITION 2 VOICINGS

The procedure for applying Open Position 2 voicings is a little different from applying Open Position 1 voicings when playing both melody and chords. When playing Open Position 2 voicings, the right hand must play a wider interval (a fourth or fifth) along with a melody note. Thus, **OPF2** is not as easily used as **OPF1** when playing melody and chords. This lesson will proceed directly to the playing of melody and chords together.

ALL THE MOON AND THINGS

Because of the open fifths played with the left hand, Open Position 2 voicings sound very rich and resonant. Because of the natural overtones produced, these voicings can be played quite low on the keyboard. The left hand voicings can sound better in a lower register than the Open Position 1 voicings. With Open Position 2 voicings the hands can be, and quite often are, more separated than with Open Position 1 voicings.

Use the following rules for playing "All The Moon and Things":

RULES: Play the root and fifth of each chord in the left hand.

Play the melody note as the uppermost note in the right hand. Build the remainder of the voicing down from the first melody note of each chord–either 3 then 7 or 7 then 3–depending on which order lies closer under the melody note.

Play each voicing only once with the first melody note of each chord. Play all other melody notes as single notes while holding down each voicing. (The damper pedal is often necessary).

The basic texture consists of a melody note plus a four-note voicing (five-note texture). It is best to keep the fifths in the left hand as low as possible without going below the first Bb or Ab below the staff.

In some cases, when a melody note is low, only a four-note texture will be possible. If the bottom note of the right hand voicing would occur below D beneath middle C, it is best to leave that note out as the sound becomes too dense. If the melody note is relatively low, there may be no room for a third note in the right hand (see measure 13).

When the first melody note with a new chord is not a chord tone, but resolves to a chord tone, leave that note of resolution out of the voicing in order for the melody to resolve to it (see measures 17 and 21).

When the first melody note of a new chord has been tied, play the remaining chord tones below while tying the melody note (see measures 18 and 22).

Fig. 17-1. All the Moon and Things

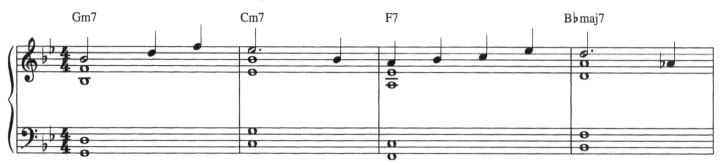

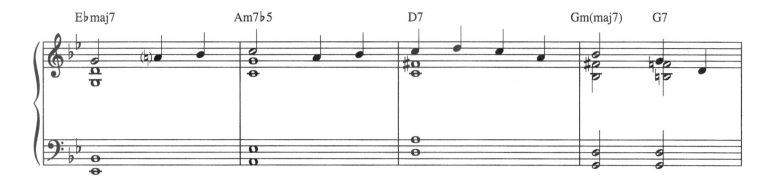

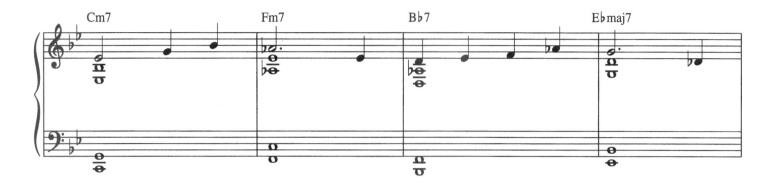

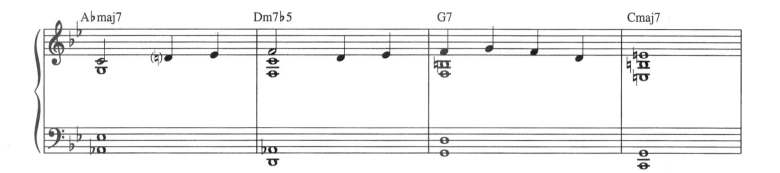

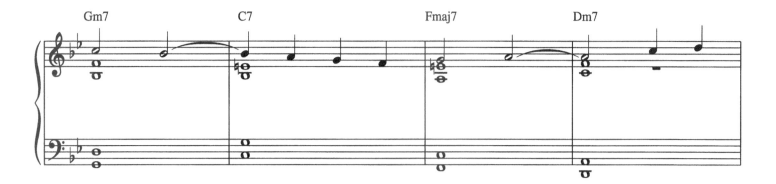

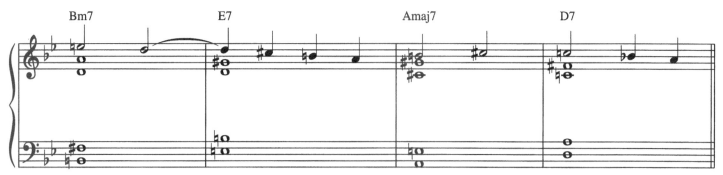

Continue...

LESSON 18
CIRCLE OF FIFTHS PROGRESSIONS
COMBINED OPEN VOICINGS

As with the closed position voicings and Open Position 1 voicings, the principles at work in **OPF2** can be applied to any root movement around the circle of descending fifths (see Lessons 6 and 15). In this instance, 1-5-3-7 voicings will alternate with 1-5-7-3 voicings. As before, a single chord quality is isolated and two cycles are presented for each example in order to accommodate all possible combinations.

I-IV PROGRESSIONS—
MAJOR SEVENTH CHORD MOVEMENT

Fig. 18-1

III-VI PROGRESSIONS—
MINOR SEVENTH CHORD MOVEMENT

Fig. 18-2

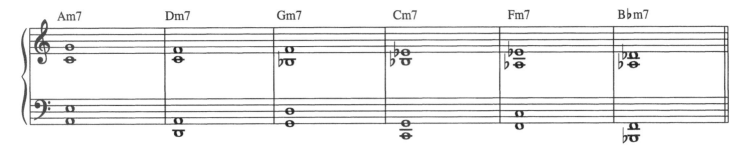

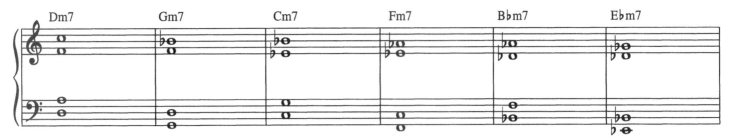

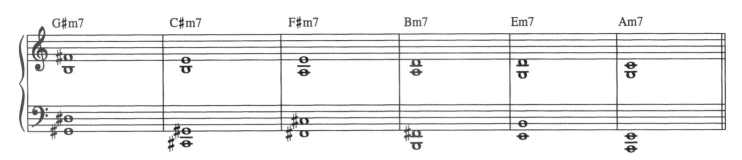

V OF V PROGRESSIONS —
DOMINANT SEVENTH CHORD MOVEMENT

Fig. 18-3

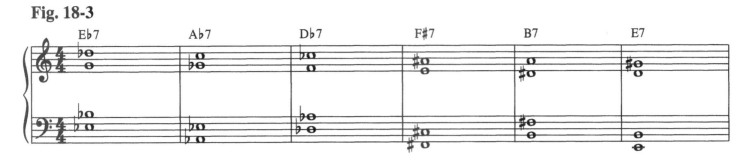

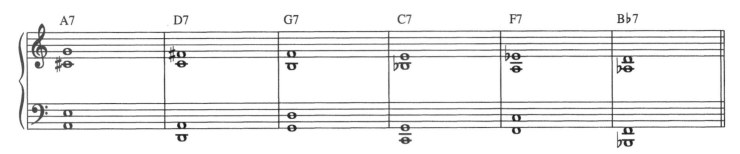

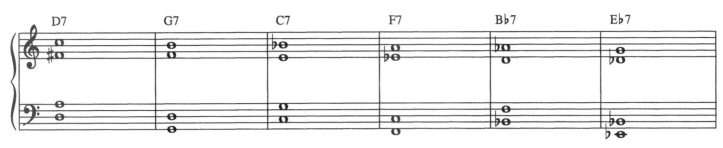

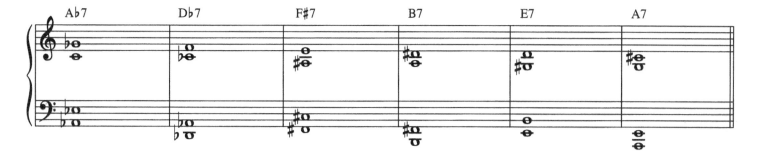

COMBINED OPEN VOICINGS
MARIA MY CHILD

In most situations a combination of voicings is desirable. By combining different voicings, variety and interest is better maintained during any given performance. As seen from the previous few lessons, certain voicings work better in certain situations. "Maria My Child" presents an opportunity to combine Open Position 1 and Open Position 2 voicings in an effective manner. The choice of voicings are determined by what sounds best and what works best within the context of the harmonic and melodic movements within the tune. Notice when and how each type of voicing is used. Study and play "Maria My Child." See p. 151 of the Appendix for the lead sheet.

The progression encountered in measures 5-6 presents a common type of harmonic movement. The first three chords in these measures have G as their root and all are a type of G minor chord. These chords give motion to an otherwise static harmonic condition by implying a motion of one voice descending by half steps. In this case the upper voice in the left hand moves down in half steps. Without this elaboration the suggested harmony is Gm7, which is part of a II-V progression coupled to C7. In this kind of situation a triad (Gm) is allowed as the first chord in order to facilitate this half step motion. Although not done here, the descending motion is often placed in the lowest voice.

Parallel 1-7-3-5 and 1-5-3-7 dominant voicings are used in measures 21 and 22 respectively to accommodate the melody. Notice the combined voicings used in the II-V-I progressions during measures 8-9, 16-17, and 31-32. Open Position 1 voicings are used for the II and V chord, but an Open Position 2 voicing is used for the I chord. Notice also the mixed voicings used in measures 23-24.

Play and study "Maria My Child."

Fig. 18-4 Maria My Child

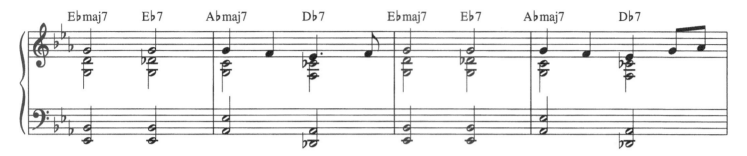

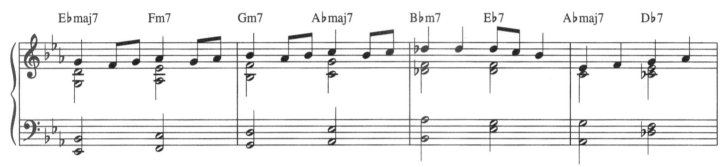

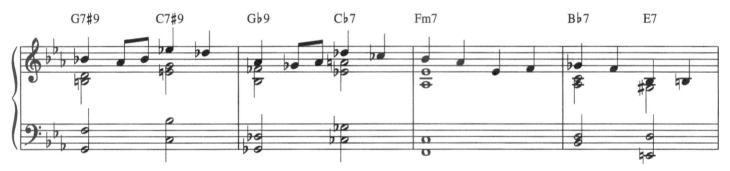

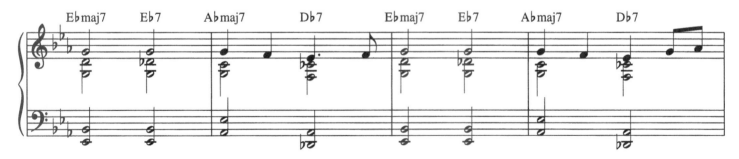

LESSON 19
OPEN VOICINGS WITH EXTENSIONS

Thus far, voicings of only four notes have been used. Often, when playing melody and chords a five-note texture (one melody note and a four-note voicing) is all that is practical. Five-note voicings *are* practical, however, when playing chords without melody. The following discussion presents five-note open position voicings based on Open Position 1 and 2 voicings. In each instance, an extra note is added to the basic voicing.

MAJOR KEYS

An extra note can easily be added to an Open Position 1 in two different ways: In the first example, a ninth is added to the II chord in the right hand *above* the 3-5 voicing. This is then held over with the other notes in the right hand and becomes the thirteenth of the V chord. All notes in the right hand then move down by step and the added voice becomes a ninth for the I chord. For the second example, a ninth is added to the II chord *below* the 3-5 voicing in the right hand. This voice functions the same way as before but as an inner voice instead of the upper voice. The second version with the added inner voice can sometimes be used when playing a melody on top, creating a six-note texture.

Fig. 19-1

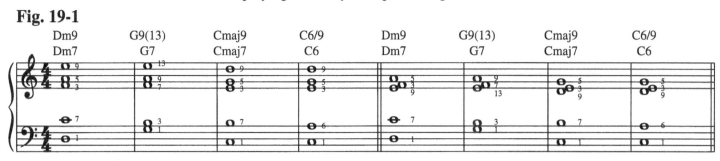

Each version of the extended chord tone Open Position Formula 1 voicings is presented below in all major keys.

Fig. 19-2

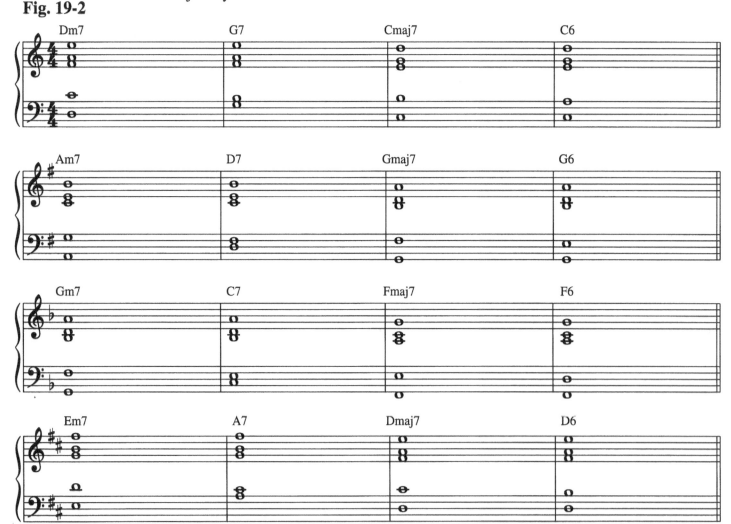

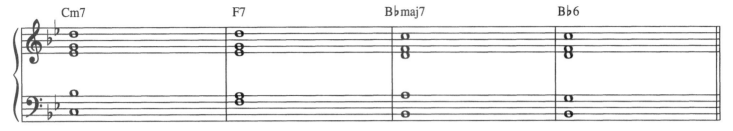

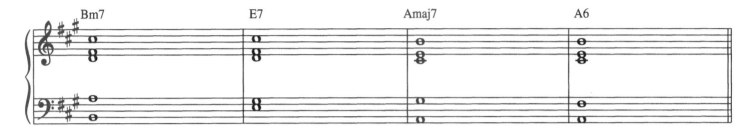

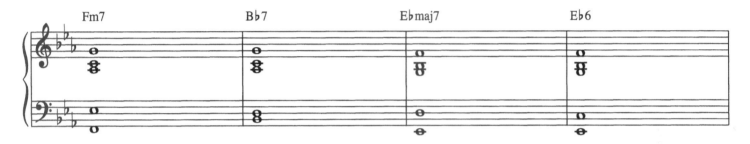

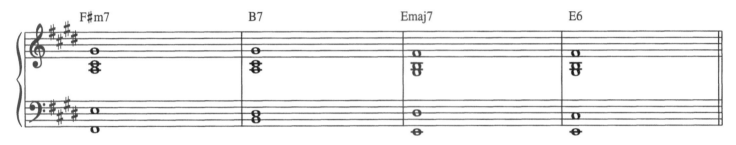

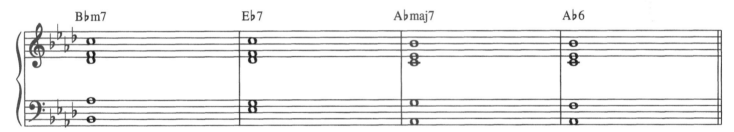

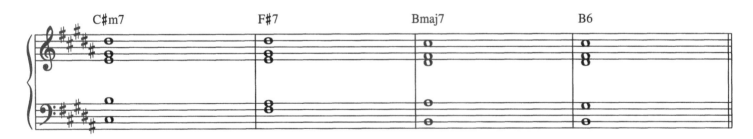

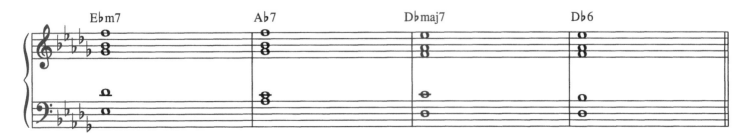

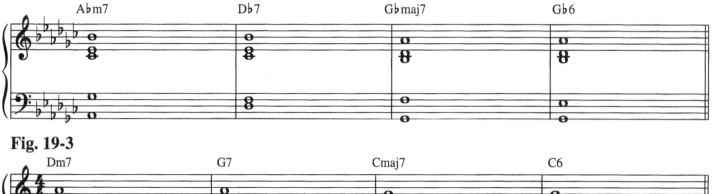

Fig. 19-3

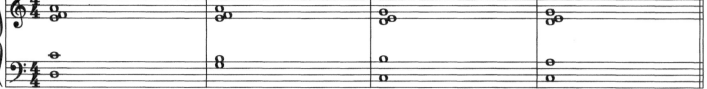

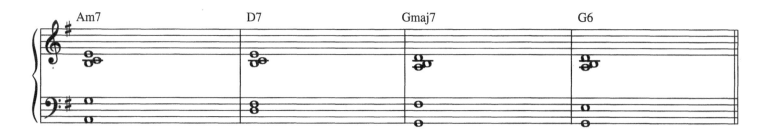

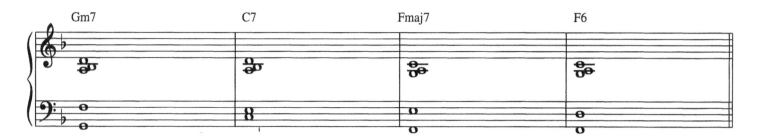

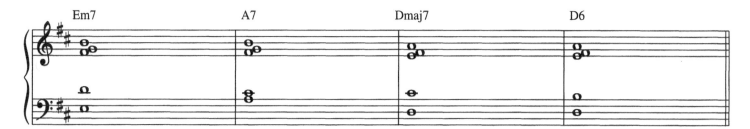

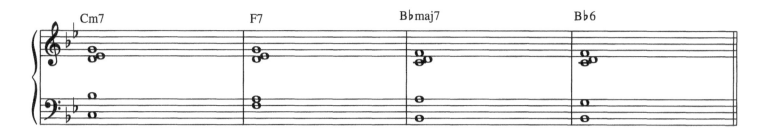

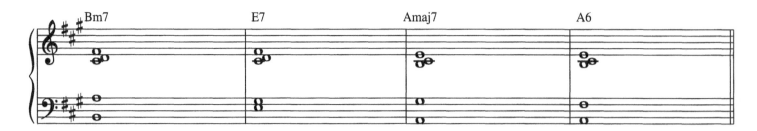

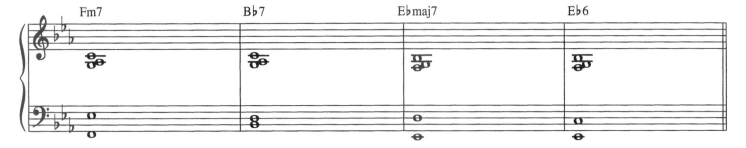

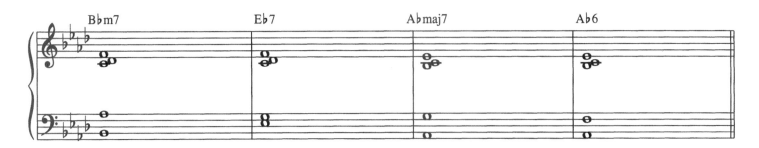

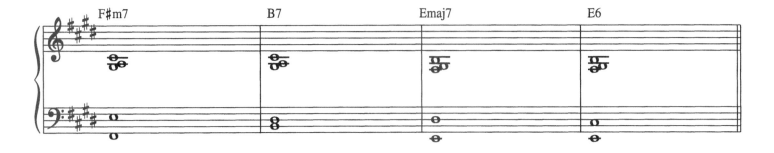

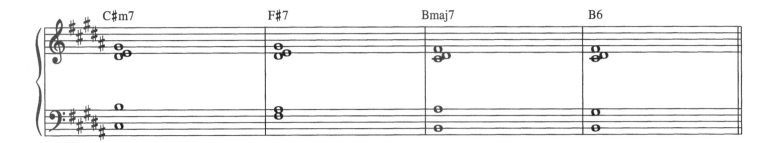

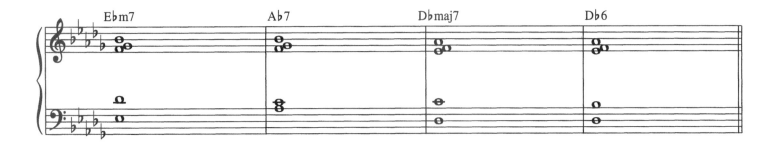

The concept of adding a fifth note to a basic voicing also applies to Open Position 2 voicings. The example below presents two possibilities, one for each alternative **OPF2** voicing presented in Lesson 16. In each case, as done previously with **OPF1**, a ninth is added to the II chord which becomes the thirteenth for the V chord. The extra voice then moves down by step and becomes the ninth of the I chord.

Fig. 19-4

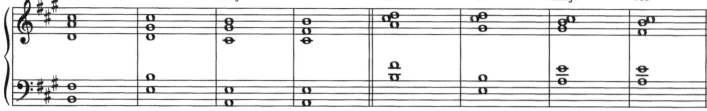

MINOR KEYS

All of the five-note voicings presented above can also be applied to minor keys. The use of chord extensions can be a problem in minor because of the lack of a consistent minor scale and diatonic chord system. Extensions are not universally applied as in major. The use of a natural nine or a flat nine, and a natural thirteenth or a flat thirteenth depends on the situation. Melody notes, written or improvised, can determine which extensions to use. Often the ninth is not used at all on a m7b5 chord and a doubling of the root is used instead.

Following are four possible applications of chord extensions for **OPF1** II-V-I progressions in minor. Both placements of the extensions are presented, as they were for major keys. Play each figure and notice the different ways that the extensions are applied.

Fig. 19-5

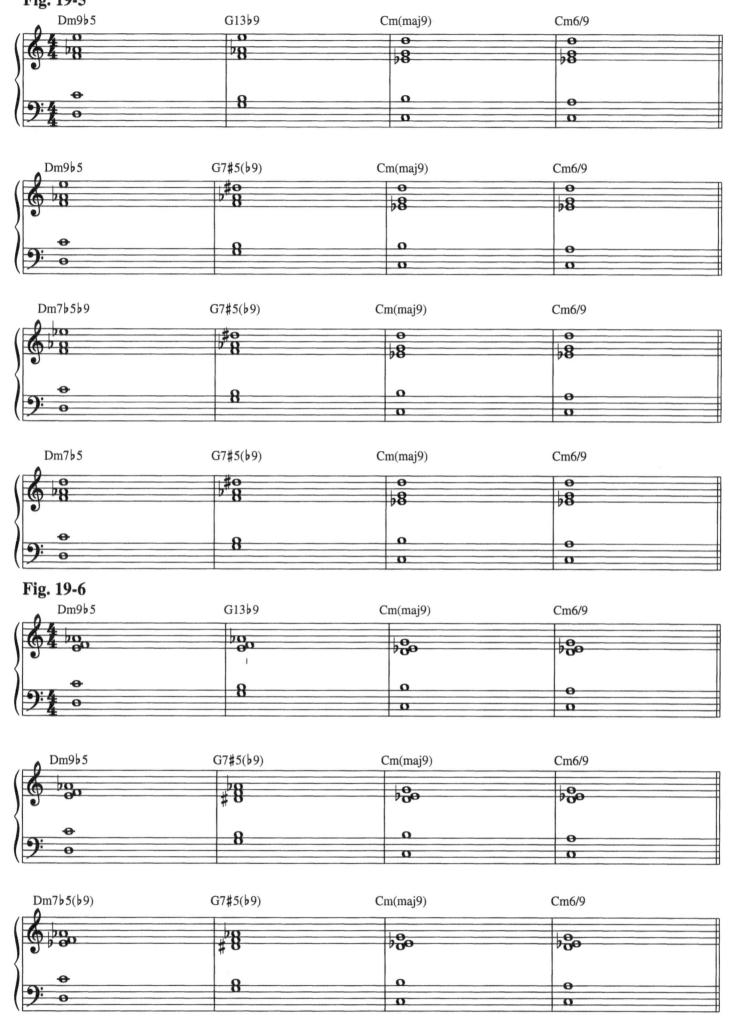

Fig. 19-6

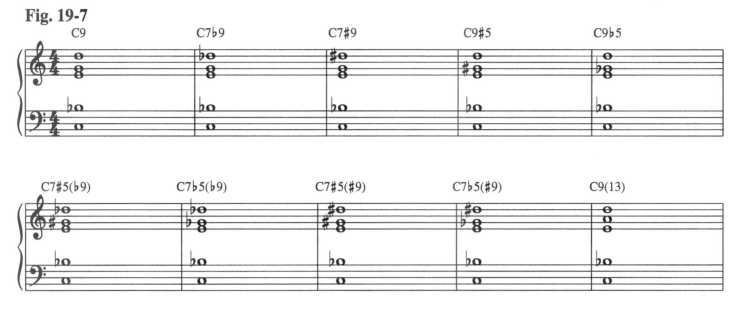

Play the above formulas in all minor keys.

Apply the same extensions to **OPF2.**

Since the five-note voicings presented above are difficult to use while playing a melody, they can, for now, be used best as accompanying chords.

Play through the chord changes of "Lunar Eclipse", "Minors Allowed," "Autumn Wonderland," and "All the Moon and Things" using chord extensions in various ways. Feel free to try as many alternatives as possible. Try flatted ninths and thirteenths as opposed to natural ninths and thirteenths.

DOMINANT VOICINGS WITH EXTENSIONS

Dominant seventh chords offer the most opportunities for chord extensions and alterations. Fifths are often altered as well as ninths, elevenths, and thirteenths. Below are examples of some possible voicings for dominant ninth chords. Notice the 1-7 or 1-5 intervals used in the left hand. See measures 21-22 of "Maria My Child" in Lesson 18 for an example of these voicings.

Fig. 19-7

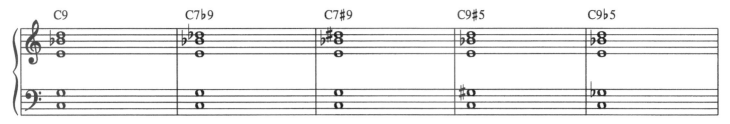

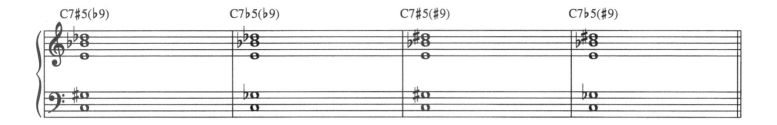

LESSON 20
ROOTLESS VOICINGS

Rootles voicings are chord voicings that do not contain the root of the chord. Letting go of the root allows for more freedom and flexibility in regard to chord alterations and extensions. Rootless voicings are also helpful when playing with a bass player. The bassist can supply the root and also substitute other notes more freely with less chance of clashing with the voicing from the pianist.

Two essential formulas for rootless voicings have evolved in jazz piano playing since the 1950s. These formulas will be presented first and several common variations will follow. As before, right hand voicings will be presented with the root in the left hand. Although the voicing contains a root in the left hand, the voicing in the right hand will still be considered as rootless.

Rootless voicings are easier to think of, and make more sense, in the context of a chord progression than as isolated chord voicings. Thus, diatonic seventh chords will not be presented here and this lesson will begin with II-V-I progressions.

ROOTLESS VOICINGS FORMULA 1
MAJOR KEYS

Rootless Voicing Formula 1 (**RVF1**) is a straightforward way of playing II-V-I progressions without roots and with chord extensions with only one hand.

Fig. 20-1

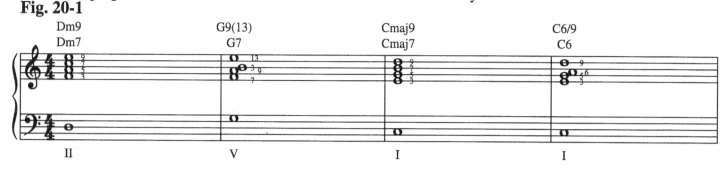

The rootless voicings are in the right hand and the root is in the left hand. Notice the extended chord tones used in the right hand. The II chord contains a ninth, the V chord contains a ninth and thirteenth, and the I chords contain a ninth. Notice that only one note moves stepwise between the II and V chords and between the I chords.

Play voicings in all keys as before and play in two cycles of descending whole steps. The following order in each cycle should be used: **C, Bb, Ab, Gb, E, D,** and **Eb, Db, B, A, G, F.** See Chapter 2. Practice Rootless Voicing Formula 1 in the following three ways:

1. RH VOICINGS
LH ROOTS

Fig. 20-2

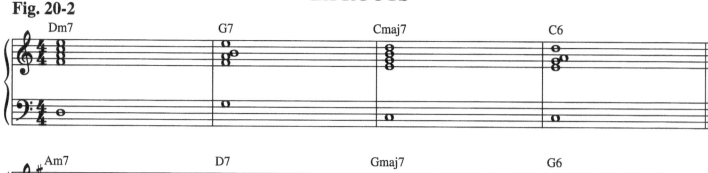

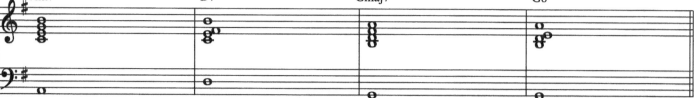

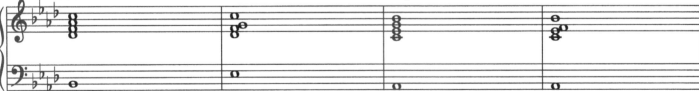

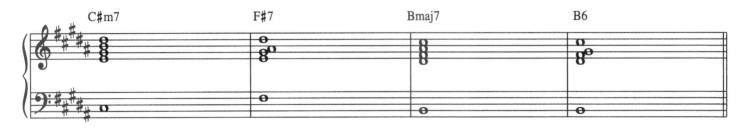

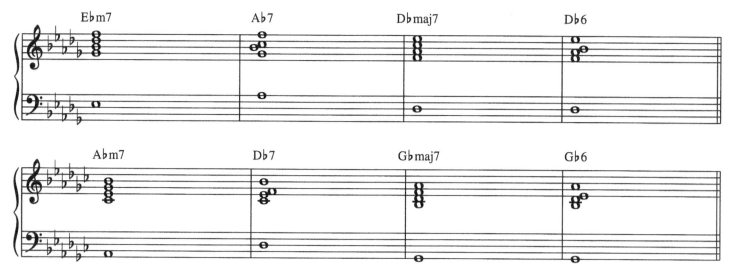

2. LH VOICINGS

Play just the voicings in the left hand as below:

Fig. 20-3

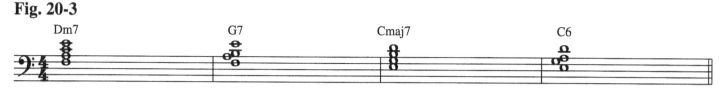

3. LH ROOT THEN LH VOICING

Play the root of each chord in the left hand and on beat three play the rootless voicing. Alternate roots and voicing for each chord as below:

Fig. 20-4

ROOTLESS VOICING FORMULA 2
MAJOR KEYS

Rootless Voicing Formula 2 (**RVF2**) contains the same notes as **RVF1** but voices them in a different order. **RVF2** voicings are inversions of **RVF1** voicings. Below is **RVF2** in the key of C major:

Fig. 20-5

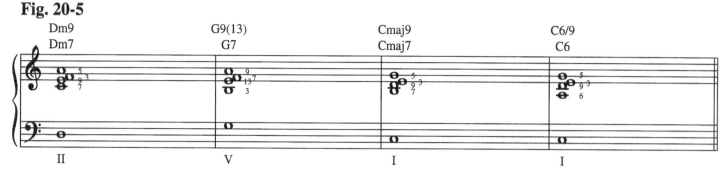

Notice that the same extensions are used as in **RVF1.** A different sound is produced with each voicing formula due to the interval structure of each voicing. **RVF2** voicings sound more tense due to the tighter spacing of the notes, especially the minor second intervals used in the II and V chord voicings.

Practice **RVF2** in the same ways as **RVF1.**

1. RH VOICINGS
LH ROOTS

Fig. 20-6

2. LH VOICINGS

Fig. 20-7

3. LH ROOT THEN VOICING

Fig. 20-8

MINOR KEYS

Since the minor key is more ambiguous than the major key, care must be used when using extended chord tones in a minor key. The same problems and alternatives discussed in Lesson 19 also apply here with rootless voicings in minor (see Lesson 19).

As before, four possible voicing formulas are presented for II-V-I progressions in minor. Examples of **RVF1** and **RVF2** in minor are given. Practice each formula in all minor keys following the same procedures as for **RVF1** and **RVF2** in major.

Fig. 20-9

Fig. 20-10

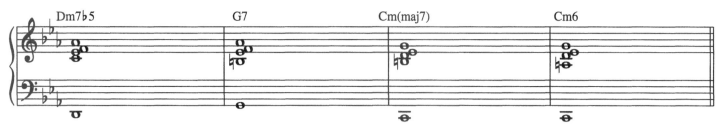

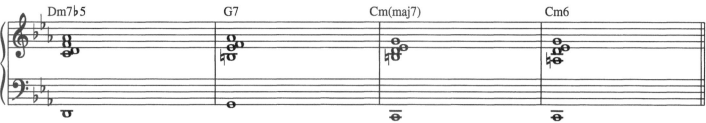

LESSON 21
APPLYING ROOTLESS VOICING FORMULAS

Rootless voicings can be used in a number of ways. A few preliminary methods are presented in this lesson. As in the earlier part of this book, melody and chords will be dealt with by separating the functions of each hand.

SPRING SWING

"Spring Swing" was discussed in Lesson 7 when Close Position Formula 1 voicings were used. The same procedures are now applied with rootless voicings.

Play "Spring Swing" in the following four ways:

1. RH VOICINGS
LH ROOTS

Play through the chord changes using both **RVF1** and **RVF2**. Notice in the example below that some progressions use **RVF1** while others use **RVF2**.

Fig. 21-1 Spring Swing

2. LH VOICINGS ALONE

Rootless voicings should not be played too low on the keyboard since they tend to sound "muddy," and/or the lowest note might be heard as a root. The lower and upper limits for a rootless voicing in the left hand should generally be between the C below middle C to the G above middle C. Of course, there are exceptions to these limits. The voicing formulas used were chosen with this principle in mind. Through experience, one will tend to use one formula over the other because of range restrictions and right hand interference.

Fig. 21-2 Spring Swing

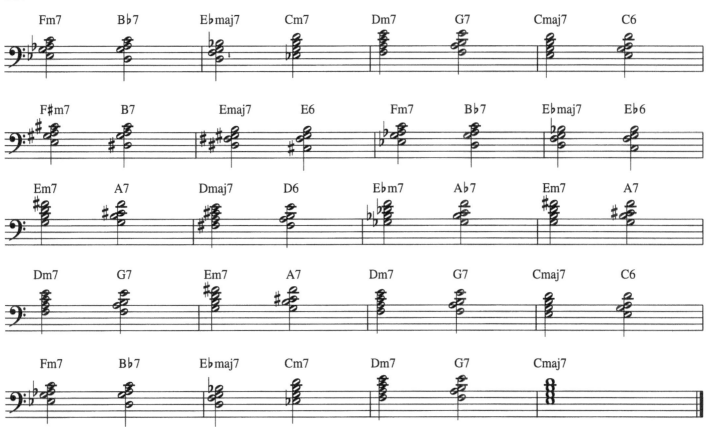

3. RH MELODY
LH VOICINGS

Play through the melody with the right hand while using rootless voicings in the left hand.

Fig. 21-3 Spring Swing

4. RH MELODY
LH VOICINGS - COMP STYLE

Play as above, but with a swing comping style (see Lesson 7) in the left hand.

Fig. 21-4 Spring Swing

Continue...

LESSON 22
COMBINED ROOTLESS VOICINGS
CIRCLE OF FIFTHS PROGRESSIONS

Rootless voicings can be used effectively for Circle of Fifths progressions in the same way that closed and open voicings were used. (see Lessons 6, 15, and 18).

In the following cycles, a **RVF1** voicing will alternate with a **RVF2** voicing and vice versa. As before, a single chord quality is isolated for each example, and each cycle represents a standard type of chord movement. Two cycles are presented for each example in order to accommodate all possible combinations.

I-IV PROGRESSIONS —
MAJOR SEVENTH CHORD MOVEMENT

In these cycles a 3-5-7-9 voicing alternates with a 7-9-3-5 voicing: Play as written and with the LH alone.

Fig. 22-1

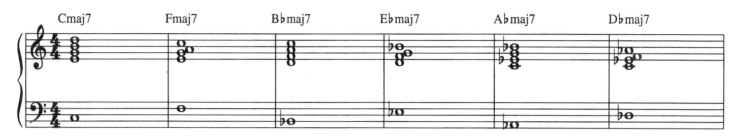

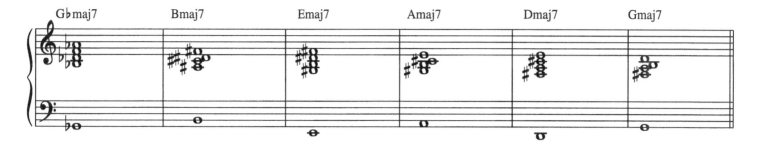

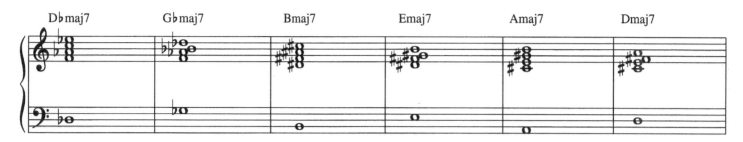

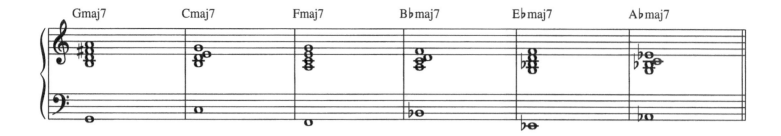

III-VI PROGRESSIONS –
MINOR SEVENTH CHORD MOVEMENT

In these cycles a 3-5-7-9 voicing alternates with a 7-9-3-5 voicing:

Fig. 22-2

V OF V PROGRESSIONS –
DOMINANT SEVENTH CHORD MOVEMENT

In these cycles a 7-9-3-13 voicing alternates with a 3-13-7-9 voicing:

Fig. 22-3

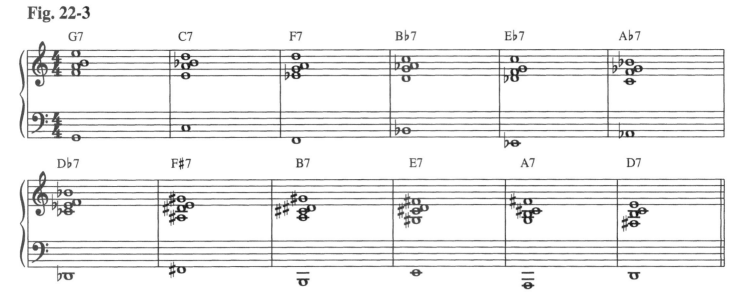

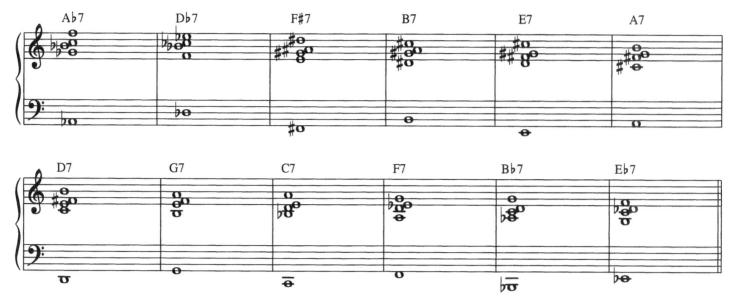

AUTUMN WONDERLAND

"Autumn Wonderland" makes use of all the progressions above.   Play "Autumn Wonderland" in the following four ways:

1. RH VOICINGS
LH ROOTS

Fig. 22-4

2. LH VOICINGS ALONE

Fig. 22-5

3. RH MELODY
LH VOICINGS

Fig. 22-6

4. RH MELODY
LH VOICINGS - COMP STYLE (SWING)

Fig. 22-7

Continue...

SUSPENSIONS

Suspensions can be created from rootless voicings in the same way they were from close position chords (see Lesson 12). A rootless voicing for a II chord (minor seventh) can be held over the root for the V chord in a II-V progression. The resulting suspended chord is technically a dominant thirteenth sus4 chord. In the key of C major this may be indicated as Fmaj7/G. The root of this chord is G. "Fmaj7" indicates the upper partials of a G7sus chord—the ninth, eleventh (same as the fourth), and the thirteenth. The chord is not an Fmaj7 chord. "Fmaj7" is a convenient way of conceptualizing the voicing.

Fig. 22-8

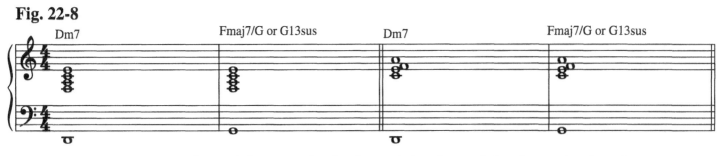

Rootless suspension voicings can be freely used in place of dominant chords, when appropriate (see Lesson 12).

ALTERED VOICINGS

Altered notes can be added to rootless voicings by adjusting notes accordingly. The examples below demonstrate some possibilities.

Fig. 22-9

Altered chord voicings can be used when indicated by the music or they can be freely employed by the player, when appropriate. Several examples of this technique will be demonstrated throughout the rest of the book. The reader should practice all of the voicings above for all twelve roots. Rootless diminished voicings can be formed by applying the same structure (adjusted) as used for minor seventh chords - min3 - dim 5 - dim7 - maj9, or dim7 - maj9 - min3 - dim5.

LESSON 23
COMBINED OPEN AND ROOTLESS VOICINGS
ARRANGING DEVICES

This arrangement of "Sunny and Soul" illustrates a professional piano styling for a medium jazz ballad. All of the arranging devices are based on Part 2 of the book. Open and rootless voicings are applied freely and the arrangement is not restricted by the use of any consistent voicing or voicing formula.

Several simple new devices are used in the arrangement. These devices provide a simple means of keeping motion going in the left hand by defining the basic quarter note pulse. Below are samples of the devices:

A. Play the root and seventh of the chord on the first beat and the fifth of the chord on the on the next beat.

Fig. 23-1A

B. Play the root of the chord on the first beat then the tenth above (same as the third but an octave higher) on the next beat.

Fig. 23-1B

C. Play the root of the chord on the first beat, the fifth of an **OPF2** voicing on the next beat.

Fig. 23-1C

D. Play the root of the chord on the first beat and the fifth on the second beat while playing a rootless voicing or fragment of a voicing in the right hand.

Fig. 23-1D

E. Play a rootless voicing then the bass note. This is a stride variation.

Fig. 23-1E

F. Play a (root and fifth) (or a root and tenth) instead of root alone and then a rootless voicing, or vice-versa as above. This is another stride variation.

Fig. 23-1F

The following is the arrangement and a measure by measure analysis of "Sunny and Soul." Study it carefully and play the arrangement. An analysis follows on p. 124.

Fig. 23-2 Sunny and Soul

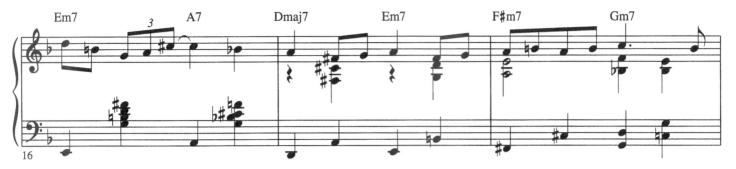

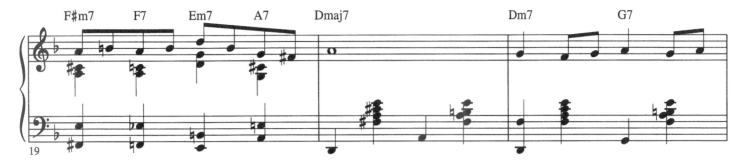

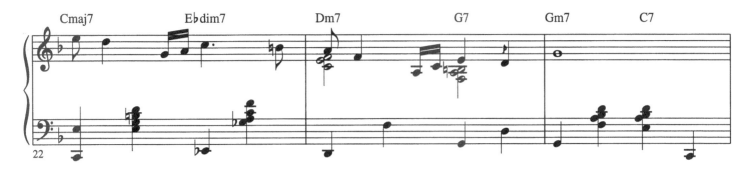

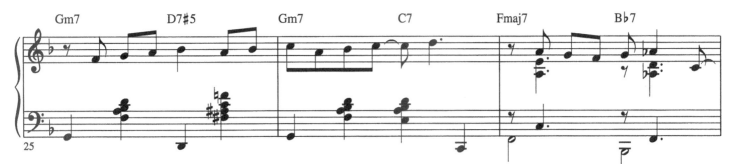

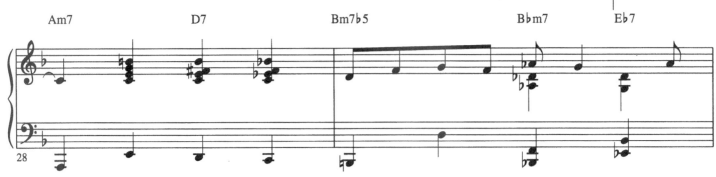

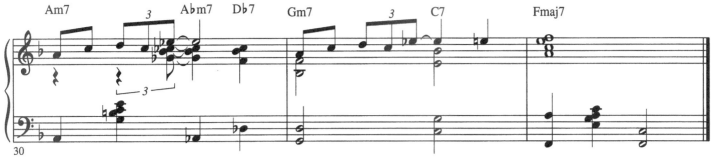

MEASURES	ARRANGING TECHNIQUE	VOICINGS
1-3	Stride-rootless	♯9♭13 voicing for D7♯5 Use of fifths in LH
4	**OPF1,** (1-7 then 5)	
5-7	Stride-rootless, **OPF1** **OPF1**	Use of root in Bm7♭5 voicing Reverse of 3-5 RH voicing
7-8	Stride-rootless	Reverse of bass note then voicing ♯9 ♭13 voicing for D7 A♭ tritone substitute for D
9	**OPF1**	use of fifth in LH
10-11	**OPF2**	
12	R then 10, rootless	Rootless voicings in RH Use of ♭9, ♭13 for D7 C as passing tone
13	R then 10, **OPF2**	Chord with melody
14	1-7 then 5, - rootless	**RVF2** in RH with melody
15	**OPF1**	
16	Stride-rootless	Use of ♭9 ♭13 for A7
17-18	**OPF2**	Separates R+5th for motion
19	**OPF1 and 2**	
20-22	Stride-rootless	Rootless diminished voicing Use of tenths in LH
23	R then 10, rootless	5th on 4th beat for motion
24-26	Stride-rootless	Reverse of bass note then voicing
27	**OPF2**	Bass then rest of voicing
28	Stride-Rootless	Use of 5th on 2nd beat for motion Passing tone and altered voicing on 4th beat
29	R then 10, **OPF2**	
30	Stride-Rootless	Rootless in LH then RH
31	**OP2**	Use of ♯9 on C7 chord
32	Stride-Rootless, 5th in LH	Close position in RH Use of tenth and fifth in LH

LESSON 24
MORE ROOTLESS VOICINGS AND APPLICATIONS

Along with the four-note rootless voicings demonstrated in the previous lessons, rootless voicings containing two, three and five notes are frequently used. This lesson will offer some possible voicings and further applications for rootless voicings.

THREE-NOTE ROOTLESS VOICINGS

Three-note rootless voicing formulas can be derived from the four-note formulas demonstrated in Lesson 20. In each case, one note is removed from each four-note voicing. Below are three-note versions of Rootless Voicing Formulas 1 and 2 (**RVF1** and **RVF2**).

Fig. 24-1

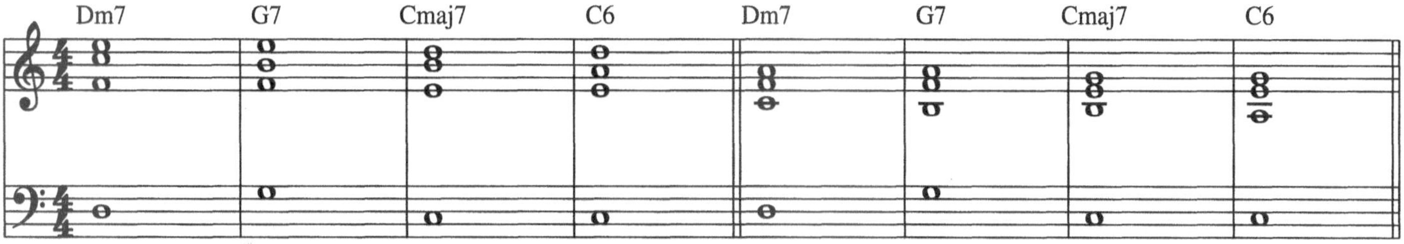

Practice the three-note formulas in all major and minor keys as before. Refer to the four-note formulas demonstrated in Lesson 20. Make all of the possible adjustments for minor.

Three-note rootless voicings should be practiced in the Circle of Fifths progressions as before. Continue the following examples for each chord quality. Refer to the four-note Circle of Fifths progressions demonstrated in Lesson 21. Practice as before with the voicing in the right hand and the root in the left hand, and with the voicing in the left hand.

Fig. 24-2

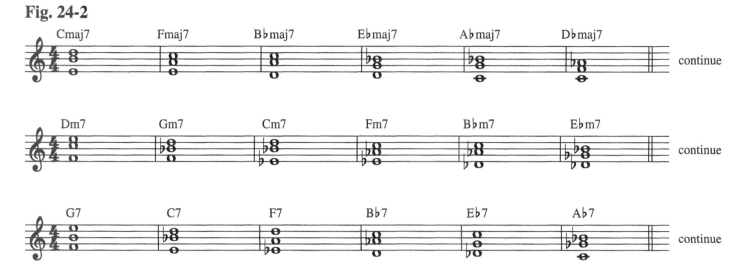

Three-note rootless voicings can be advantageous because of their ambiguity. A single voicing can be applied to different chords. The three-note structure below can be used as a voicing for G7, Db7#9, Dm6, Ddim7, Fdim7, Abdim7, and Bdim7.

Fig. 24-3

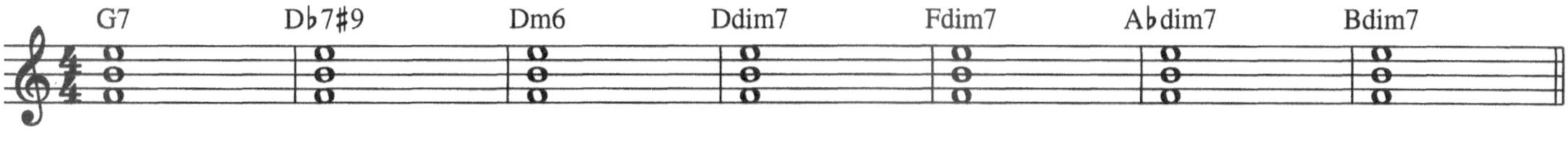

The dual dominant function (G7 and D♭7♯9) of the previous voicing can be exploited to good effect. The principle of tritone substitution is at work here, since a G7 and a D♭7 can usually substitute for each other. The example below shows how a change in bass note can effect the root function of the voicing.

Fig. 24-4

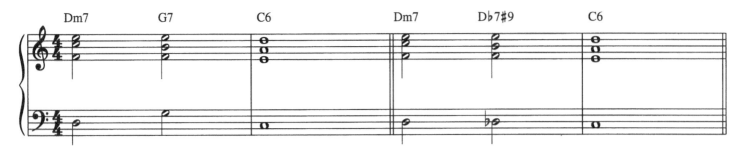

The example below demonstrates how the three-note dominant voicing used above can imply two different dominant chords. The voicing can be played in descending half steps while a root can descend either by half step or perfect fifth. When the roots descend in half steps, the chord tones of the voicing (7-3-13) move in parallel. When the roots descend by fifth, the chord tones alternate between 7-3-13 and 3-7-♯9. Some of the ♯9's are enharmonically simplified.

Fig. 24-5
Descending Half Steps

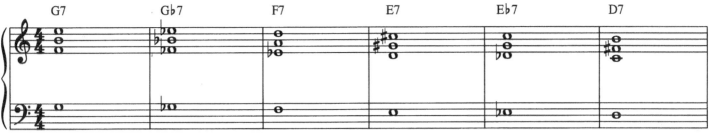

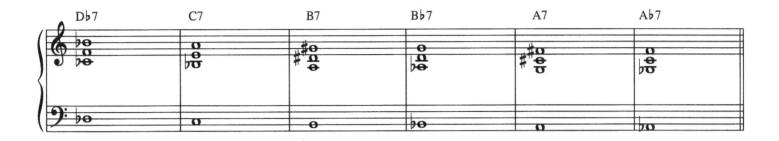

Descending Fifths

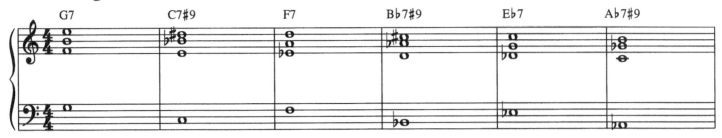

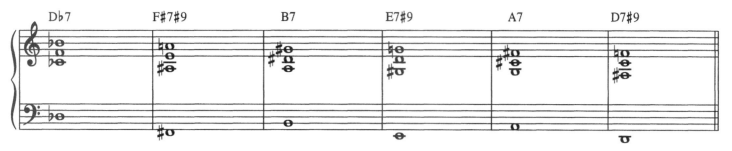

The same process can be applied to the same voicing by changing the roots to their tritone substitutes—G becomes D♭, G♭ becomes C, etc. A series of dominant seventh sharp nine chords result from the descending half step cycle and alternating dominant and dominant sharp–nine chords result from the descending fifths cycle.

Fig. 24-6
Descending Half Steps

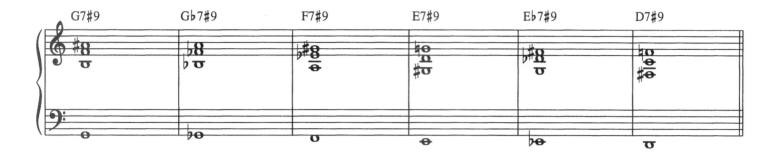

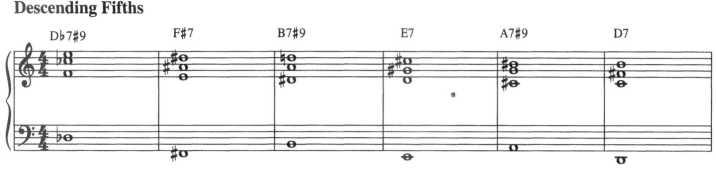

Descending Fifths

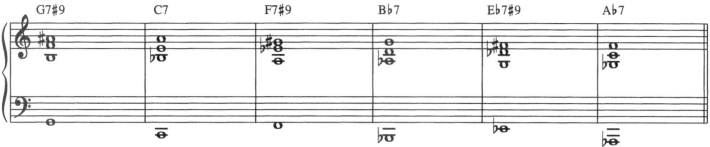

Alterations can be made to the three-note dominant voicing by adjusting the appropriate chord tone. Refer to the altered four-note rootless voicing in Lesson 23.

TWO–NOTE VOICINGS

Dominant chords can be voiced effectively with just two notes. The third and the seventh are the notes that define the dominant quality of a chord. These two notes alone can suffice for a dominant seventh chord voicing. The third and seventh of a dominant seventh chord form the interval of a tritone and the same tritone notes are found in dominant seventh chords that are a tritone apart when enharmonically adjusted. This similarity is what makes tritone substitiution of dominant seventh chords work so well. Below are two cycles of similar tritones that imply different dominant seventh chords when spelled differently.

Fig. 24-7

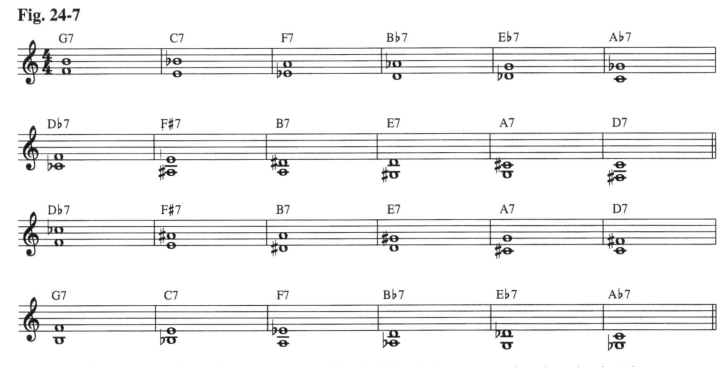

Two-note rootless voicings can be used for II-V-I and other progressions by using just the thirds and sevenths (or sixths) of any chord quality. II-V-I progressions can be voiced as below. These voicings are the same voicings that were used in the right hand for Open Position Formula 2 (see Lesson 16).

Fig. 24-8

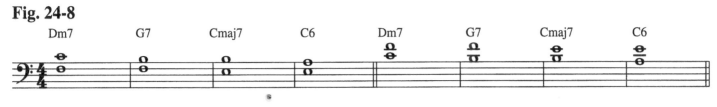

THREE–NOTE FRAGMENTS

Fragments that do not contain all essential chord tones (roots, thirds, and flatted fifths) are often used in place of other three and four-note rootless voicings. These fragments most often contain a second (usually a minor second) as the interval between the two lowest notes. Below are typical fragments used for some basic chord qualities for the root C.

Fig. 24-9

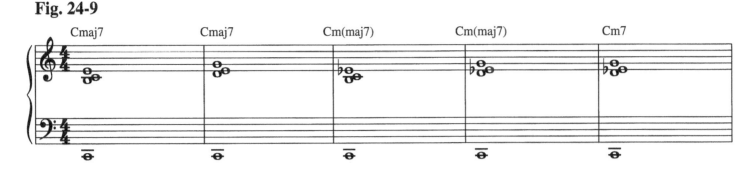

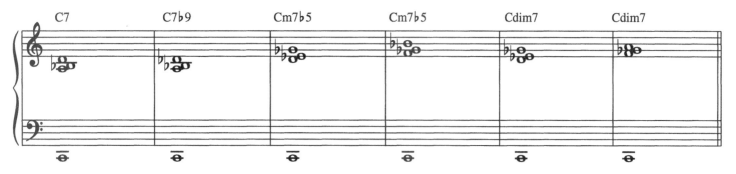

Three-note fragments are ambiguous by themselves but gain a function and syntax with an added or implied root. The example below demonstrates two different fragments with various roots and functions. The first fragments contain a minor second between the lowest notes and a major third between the upper two notes. The second fragment contains a minor second between the lowest notes and a minor third between the upper two notes.

Fig. 24-10

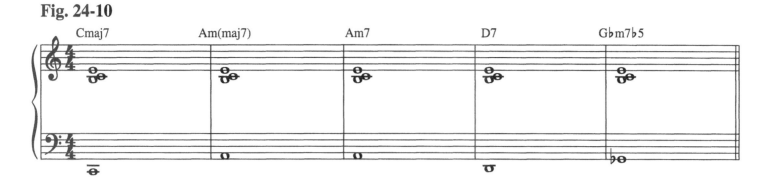

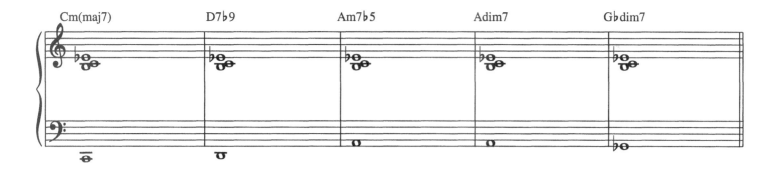

Fragments can be practiced by isolationg a chord quality for each root as shown above. Fragments can also be practiced by using them in place of other rootless voicings in rootless voicing formulas and cycles. Below are a few samples:

Fig. 24-11

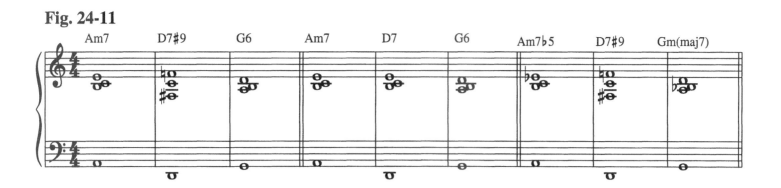

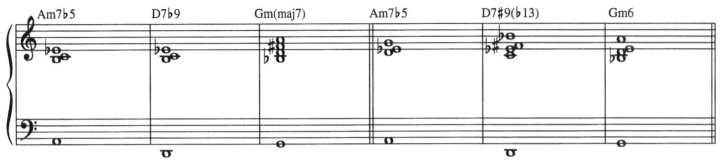

FIVE-NOTE ROOTLESS VOICINGS

Two notes are often added to the standard three-note rootless voicings to produce a five-note open voicing. The two notes are a perfect fourth apart and are added a perfect fourth above a three-note rootless voicing. The interval structure of these voicings emphasize the sound of open fourths. Below is a sample of five-note rootless voicings based on Rootless Voicing Formulas 1 and 2. Although the root appears as an upper voice in some voicings, it does not function as a root because of its placement in the chord. These voicings are considered to be rootless.

Fig. 24-12

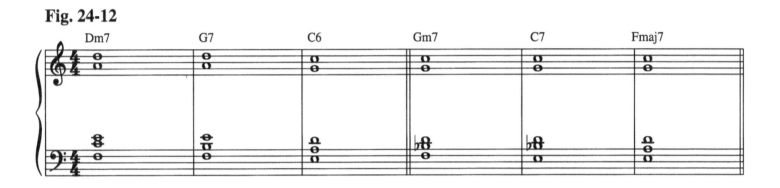

Practice in all major keys as before. Minor keys do not work as smoothly as major keys when using this system. Minor formulas can be skipped for the present, although isolated five-note rootless voicings can work well in minor. You will notice that because of range limitations one or the other voicing formula will work better with each major key since they are spread out so much. These voicings can be played only with both hands.

Five-note rootless voicing can be practiced as before by isolating separate qualities in a Circle of Fifths progression. Continue the examples below as in Lesson 22.

Fig. 24-13

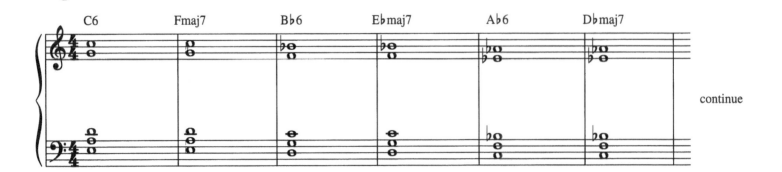

continue

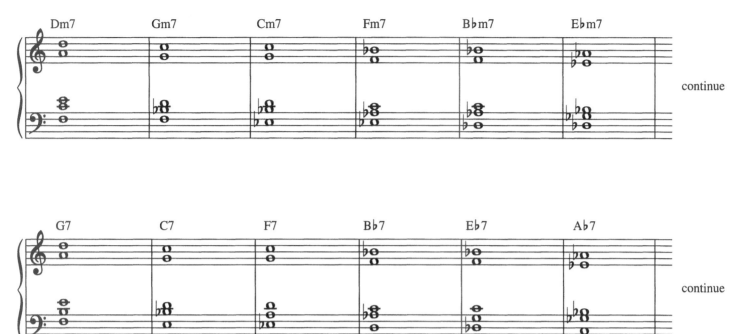

continue

continue

The five-note voicings demonstrated here are most easily used for comping but can also be employed in a full two-handed piano arragement when used carefully.

APPLICATIONS

The following examples apply the voicings demonstrated in this lesson along with previously learned voicings. Play through the examples and complete each tune in a similar manner when necessary. Study and analyze each example and apply the same ideas to other tunes.

ALL THE MOON AND THINGS

Fig. 24-14

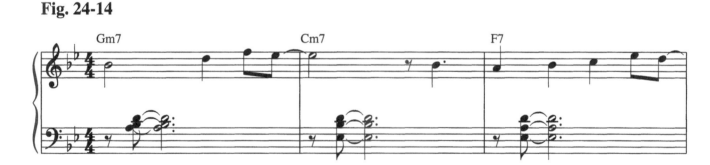

continue

HOMILY

Fig. 24-15

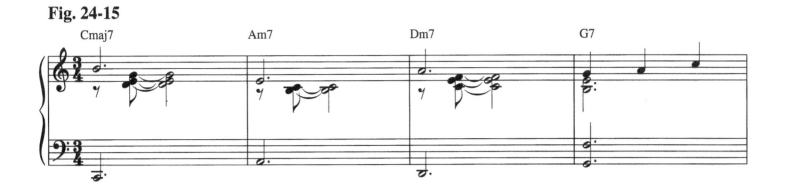

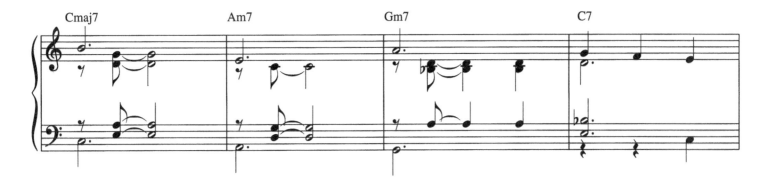

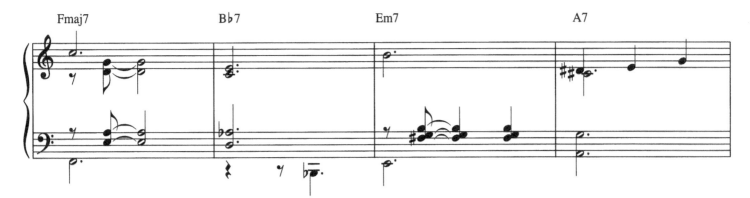

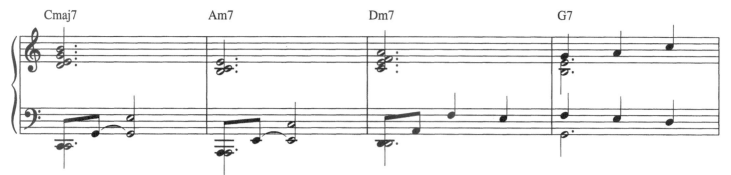

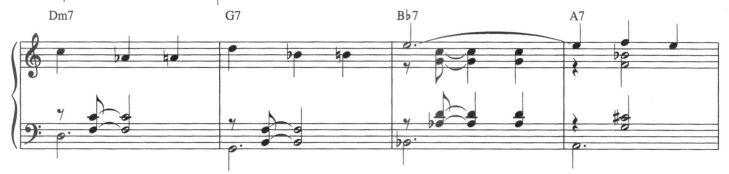

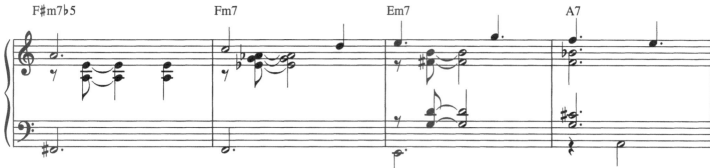

BOSSATION

Fig. 24-16

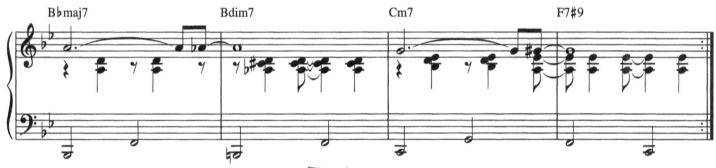

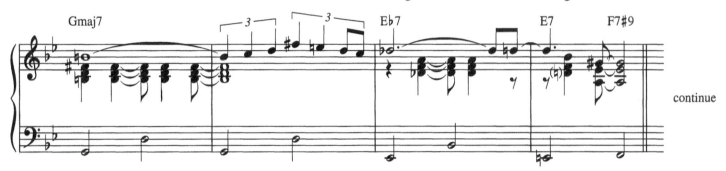

continue

APPENDIX
MAJOR SCALES

MINOR SCALES

B Natural Minor

B Harmonic Minor

B Melodic Minor (ascending)

B Melodic Minor (descending)

G Natural Minor

G Harmonic Minor

G Melodic Minor (ascending)

G Melodic Minor (descending)

F♯ Natural Minor

F♯ Harmonic Minor

F♯ Melodic Minor (ascending)

F♯ Melodic Minor (descending)

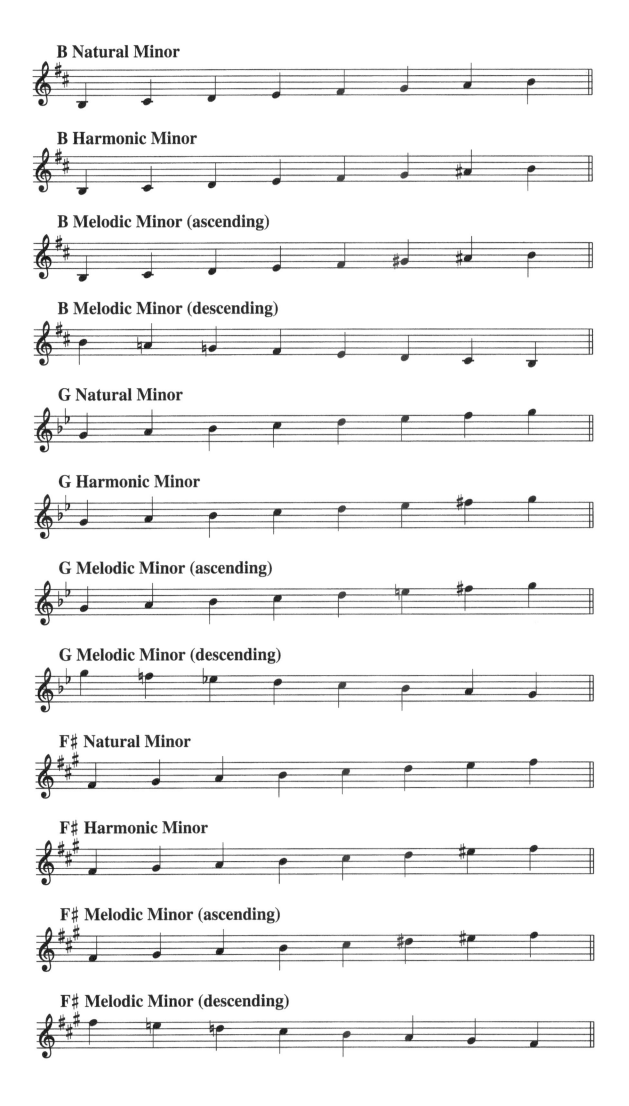

C Natural Minor

C Harmonic Minor

C Melodic Minor (ascending)

C Melodic Minor (descending)

C# Natural Minor

C# Harmonic Minor

C# Melodic Minor (ascending)

C# Melodic Minor (descending)

F Natural Minor

F Harmonic Minor

F Melodic Minor (ascending)

F Melodic Minor (descending)

139

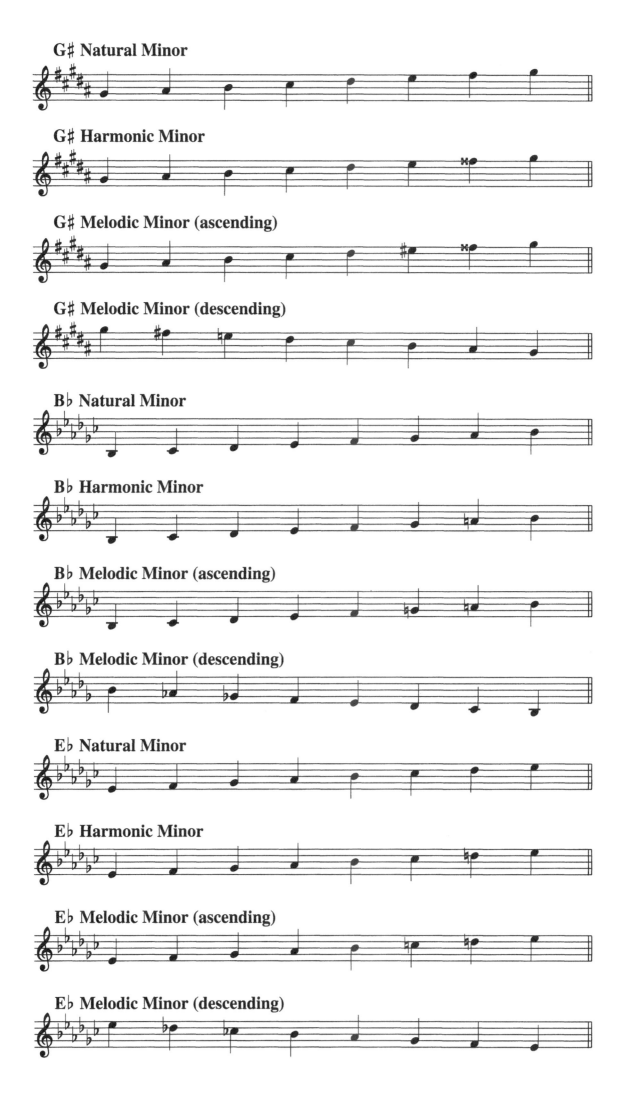

DIATONIC SEVENTH CHORDS
MAJOR KEYS

E♭ Major

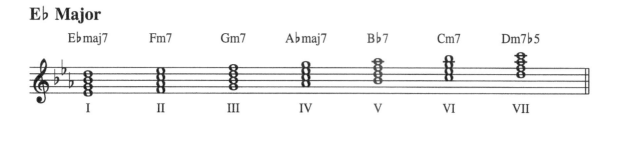

Ebmaj7   Fm7   Gm7   Abmaj7   Bb7   Cm7   Dm7b5

I   II   III   IV   V   VI   VII

E Major

Emaj7   F#m7   G#m7   Amaj7   B7   C#m7   D#m7b5

I   II   III   IV   V   VI   VII

A♭ Major

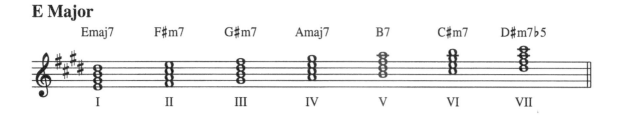

Abmaj7   Bbm7   Cm7   Dbmaj7   Eb7   Fm7   Gm7b5

I   II   III   IV   V   VI   VII

B Major

Bmaj7   C#m7   D#m7   Emaj7   F#7   G#m7   A#m7b5

I   II   III   IV   V   VI   VII

D♭ Major

Dbmaj7   Ebm7   Fm7   Gbmaj7   Ab7   Bbm7   Cm7b5

I   II   III   IV   V   VI   VII

G♭ Major

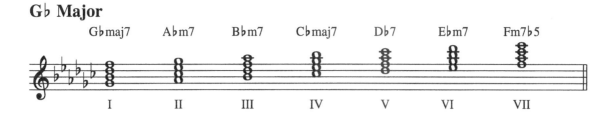

Gbmaj7   Abm7   Bbm7   Cbmaj7   Db7   Ebm7   Fm7b5

I   II   III   IV   V   VI   VII

DIATONIC SEVENTH CHORDS
MINOR KEYS

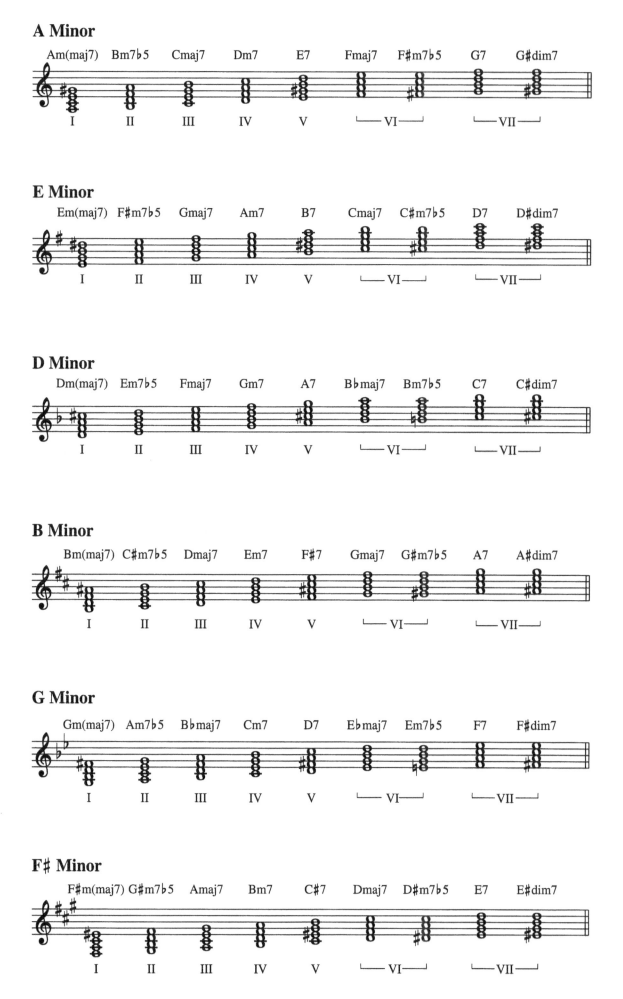

C Minor

Cm(maj7) Dm7♭5 E♭maj7 Fm7 G7 A♭maj7 Am7♭5 B♭7 Bdim7

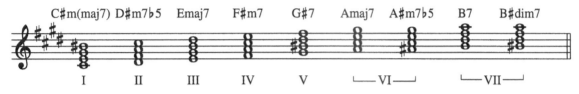

I II III IV V └── VI ──┘ └── VII ──┘

C♯ Minor

C♯m(maj7) D♯m7♭5 Emaj7 F♯m7 G♯7 Amaj7 A♯m7♭5 B7 B♯dim7

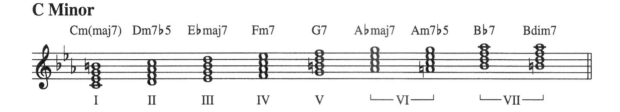

I II III IV V └── VI ──┘ └── VII ──┘

F Minor

Fm(maj7) Gm7♭5 A♭maj7 B♭m7 C7 D♭maj7 Dm7♭5 E♭7 Edim7

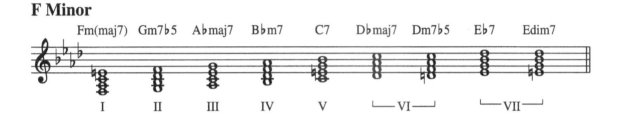

I II III IV V └── VI ──┘ └── VII ──┘

G♯ Minor

G♯m(maj7) A♯m7♭5 Bmaj7 C♯m7 D♯7 Emaj7 Fm7♭5 F♯7 Gdim7

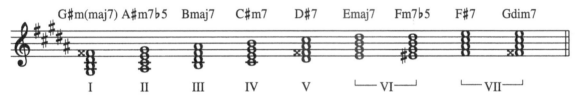

I II III IV V └── VI ──┘ └── VII ──┘

B♭ Minor

B♭m(maj7) Cm7♭5 D♭maj7 E♭m7 F7 G♭maj7 Gm7♭5 A♭7 Adim7

I II III IV V └── VI ──┘ └── VII ──┘

E♭ Minor

E♭m(maj7) Fm7♭5 G♭maj7 A♭m7 B♭7 C♭maj7 Cm7♭5 D♭7 Ddim7

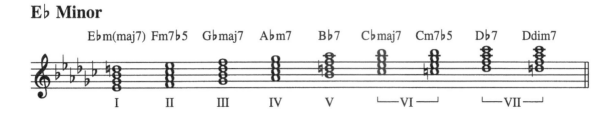

I II III IV V └── VI ──┘ └── VII ──┘

MINORS ALLOWED

HOMILY

LUNAR ECLIPSE

SPRING SWING

ALL THE MOON AND THINGS

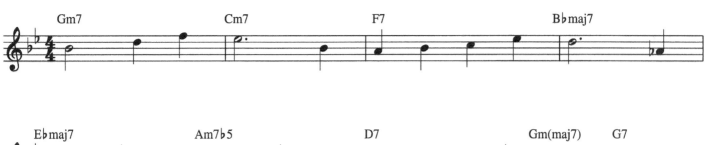

AUTUMN WONDERLAND

SUNNY AND SOUL

MARIA MY CHILD

BOSSATION